TAPESTRY

Writing 4

A Revised Edition of
The Newbury House Guide to Writing

....

M. E. Sokolik

HEINLE & HEINLE
THOMSON LEARNING

United States • Australia • Canada • Mexico • Singapore • Spain • United Kingdom

For my Mother, another book for the shelf

HEINLE & HEINLE

THOMSON LEARNING

Developmental Editors: Jennifer Monaghan, Jill Korey O'Sullivan
Sr. Production Coordinator: Maryellen E. Killeen
Market Development Director: Charlotte Sturdy
Sr. Manufacturing Coordinator: Mary Beth Hennebury
Interior Design: Julia Gecha
Illustrations: Pre-Press Company, Inc., Antonio Castro
Photo Research: Martha Friedman

Cover Design: Ha Nguyen Design
Cover Images: PhotoDisc®
Composition/Production: Pre-Press Company, Inc.
Freelance Production Editor: Janet McCartney
Copyeditor: Donald Pharr
Printer/Binder: Bawden

For permission to use material from this text, contact us:
web   www.thomsonrights.com
fax   1-800-730-2215
phone   1-800-730-2214

For photo credits, see page 224.

Heinle & Heinle Publishers
20 Park Plaza
Boston, MA 02116

UK/EUROPE/MIDDLE EAST:
Thomson Learning
Berkshire House
168-173 High Holborn
London, WC1V 7AA, United Kingdom

AUSTRALIA/NEW ZEALAND:
Nelson/Thomson Learning
102 Dodds Street
South Melbourne
Victoria 3205 Australia

CANADA:
Nelson/Thomson Learning
1120 Birchmount Road
Scarborough, Ontario
Canada M1K 5G4

LATIN AMERICA:
Thomson Learning
Seneca, 53
Colonia Polanco
11560 México D.F. México

ASIA (excluding Japan):
Thomson Learning
60 Albert Street #15-01
Albert Complex
Singapore 189969

JAPAN:
Thomson Learning
Palaceside Building, 5F
1-1-1 Hitotsubashi, Chiyoda-ku
Tokyo 100 0003, Japan

SPAIN:
Thomson Learning
Calle Magallanes, 25
28015-Madrid
España

Library of Congress Cataloging-in-Publication Data
Sokolik, M. E. (Margaret E.)
  Tapestry writing 4 / M. E. Sokolik.
    p. cm.
  ISBN 0-8384-0045-0 (alk. paper)
  1. English language—Textbooks for foreign speakers. 2. English
language—Rhetoric—Problems, exercises, etc. 3. Report writing—Problems, exercises,
etc. I. Title: Tapestry writing four. II. Title.

PE1128 .S5947 2000
808'.042—dc21   99-054094

 This book is printed on acid-free recycled paper.

Printed in the United States of America.
2 3 4 5 6 7 8 9 03 02 01 00

A VERY SPECIAL THANK YOU

The publisher and authors would like to thank the following coordinators and instructors who have offered many helpful insights and suggestions for change throughout the development of the new *Tapestry*.

Alicia Aguirre, *Cañada College*
Fred Allen, *Mission College*
Maya Alvarez-Galvan, *University of Southern California*
Geraldine Arbach, *Collège de l'Outaouais, Canada*
Dolores Avila, *Pasadena City College*
Sarah Bain, *Eastern Washington University*
Kate Baldus, *San Francisco State University*
Fe Baran, *Chabot College*
Gail Barta, *West Valley College*
Karen Bauman, *Biola University*
Liza Becker, *Mt. San Antonio College*
Leslie Biaggi, *Miami-Dade Community College*
Andrzej Bojarczak, *Pasadena City College*
Nancy Boyer, *Golden West College*
Glenda Bro, *Mt. San Antonio College*
Brooke Brummitt, *Palomar College*
Linda Caputo, *California State University, Fresno*
Alyce Campbell, *Mt. San Antonio College*
Barbara Campbell, *State University of New York, Buffalo*
Robin Carlson, *Cañada College*
Ellen Clegg, *Chapman College*
Karin Cintron, *Aspect ILS*
Diane Colvin, *Orange Coast College*
Martha Compton, *University of California, Irvine*
Nora Dawkins, *Miami-Dade Community College*
Beth Erickson, *University of California, Davis*
Charles Estus, *Eastern Michigan University*
Gail Feinstein Forman, *San Diego City College*
Jeffra Flaitz, *University of South Florida*
Kathleen Flynn, *Glendale Community College*
Ann Fontanella, *City College of San Francisco*
Sally Gearhart, *Santa Rosa Junior College*
Alice Gosak, *San José City College*
Kristina Grey, *Northern Virginia Community College*
Tammy Guy, *University of Washington*
Gail Hamilton, *Hunter College*
Patty Heiser, *University of Washington*
Virginia Heringer, *Pasadena City College*

Catherine Hirsch, *Mt. San Antonio College*
Helen Huntley, *West Virginia University*
Nina Ito, *California State University, Long Beach*
Patricia Jody, *University of South Florida*
Diana Jones, *Angloamericano, Mexico*
Loretta Joseph, *Irvine Valley College*
Christine Kawamura, *California State University, Long Beach*
Gregory Keech, *City College of San Francisco*
Kathleen Keesler, *Orange Coast College*
Daryl Kinney, *Los Angeles City College*
Maria Lerma, *Orange Coast College*
Mary March, *San José State University*
Heather McIntosh, *University of British Columbia, Canada*
Myra Medina, *Miami-Dade Community College*
Elizabeth Mejia, *Washington State University*
Cristi Mitchell, *Miami-Dade Community College*
Sylvette Morin, *Orange Coast College*
Blanca Moss, *El Paso Community College*
Karen O'Neill, *San José State University*
Bjarne Nielsen, *Central Piedmont Community College*
Katy Ordon, *Mission College*
Luis Quesada, *Miami-Dade Community College*
Gustavo Ramírez Toledo, *Colegio Cristóbol Colón, Mexico*
Nuha Salibi, *Orange Coast College*
Alice Savage, *North Harris College*
Dawn Schmid, *California State University, San Marcos*
Mary Kay Seales, *University of Washington*
Denise Selleck, *City College of San Francisco*
Gail Slater, *Brooklyn and Staten Island Superintendency*
Susanne Spangler, *East Los Angeles College*
Karen Stanley, *Central Piedmont Community College*
Sara Storm, *Orange Coast College*
Margaret Teske, *ELS Language Centers*
Maria Vargas-O'Neel, *Miami-Dade Community College*
James Wilson, *Mt. San Antonio College and Pasadena City College*
Karen Yoshihara, *Foothill College*

ACKNOWLEDGMENTS

Thanks to Erik Rogers for his assistance in developing the instructor's manual and for his insightful comments on the discussion questions. Thanks also to Jill Kinkade for her help with the CNN video. I would especially like to thank Erik Gundersen for his capable and thoughtful guidance throughout the development of this series. Finally, and most importantly, love and thanks to Jim Duber for his support and help throughout this writing/editing process.

Tapestry Writing 4: Contents

ACADEMIC POWER STRATEGIES	CNN VIDEO CLIPS	GRAMMAR YOU CAN USE	FROM READING TO WRITING
Keep a journal in order to develop your writing ideas.	"National Spelling Bee" A reporter explains who participates in spelling bees and how they are organized.	Subject-verb agreement	Reading 1: an explanation of freewriting Reading 2: an interview with a writer about journal writing Reading 3: a poem about the motivation for writing **Writing Activity:** An essay explaining your motivation for writing and your writing techniques
Discover the resources on campus and in your community for research.	"Mother Teresa" A look at the life and accomplishments of one individual who made a difference.	Avoiding sentence fragments	Reading 1: a biography about Albert Einstein Reading 2: a biography about Mother Teresa Reading 3: a biography about Jules Verne written by a student **Writing Activity:** A biographical essay about a person of your choice
Learn to use dictionaries effectively to help you in all areas of your studies.	"Ice Hotel" A description of an unusual hotel located in the Arctic Circle.	Avoiding and fixing run-ons, comma splices, and misused conjunctions	Reading 1: a description of children's secret places Reading 2: a description of the Bilbao Guggenheim museum **Writing Activity:** A descriptive essay about a building of your choice
Take notes effectively to learn more efficiently and to remember more of your learning.	"The Iditarod Race" An explanation of the history of this race and what it takes to win it.	Articles	Reading 1: an explanation of the process involved with using chopsticks Reading 2: an explanation of the process that led to the formation of the earth's moon **Writing Activity:** A paper explaining a process you know well
Find experts and sources in your community to help you locate information you need to succeed in your studies.	"The Triple Trailer Truck" A discussion of the potential danger of these large vehicles contrasted with their advantages to businesses.	Parallel structures	Reading 1: an evaluation of the advantages of leasing business equipment versus buying it Reading 2: an evaluation of the disadvantages of leasing equipment **Writing Activity:** An essay comparing and contrasting objects or services of your choice

CHAPTER	WRITING SKILLS FOCUS	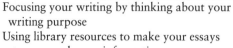 LANGUAGE LEARNING STRATEGIES
6 Informing: Diseases that Affect Us Page 96 	Focusing your writing by thinking about your writing purpose Using library resources to make your essays stronger and more informative Using prepositions correctly	Think about the purposes for writing to write in a more focused way. Use library resources to make your essays stronger and more informative.
7 Researching: Getting to the Source Page 120 	Avoiding plagiarism in all of your writing Writing effective conclusions Developing a clear point of view in your research writing Using quotations effectively and correctly	Develop a clear point of view in your research writing to make it more interesting. Learn to write effective conclusions in order to make your writing more effective.
8 Analyzing: All in the Family Page 138 	Writing effective thesis statements for analytical writing Using specialized vocabulary in your writing Making paragraphs coherent and unified	Use specialized vocabulary to write about literature more precisely. Write a strong thesis statement to make your writing clear.
9 Persuading: Making a Case Page162 	Examining writing for important features you have learned Understanding common problems and pitfalls in persuasive writing Eliminating wordiness in your writing	Examine writing for important features you have learned. Understand common problems and pitfalls in persuasive writing.
10 Proposing: The Science of Business, the Business of Science Page 186 	Understanding and using proper writing formats in workplace communication Understanding the appropriate types of address required in business writing Using spelling rules to avoid mistakes in spelling	Understand and use proper writing formats in workplace communication to succeed in your communication goal. Understand the appropriate types of address required in business writing.

ACADEMIC POWER STRATEGIES	CNN VIDEO CLIPS	GRAMMAR YOU CAN USE	FROM READING TO WRITING
Familiarize yourself with what is in your library to do research more efficiently in all your classes.	"Panic Disorder" An explanation of panic attacks, who is most likely to suffer them, and what can be done to treat them.	Prepositions	Reading 1: an informative essay on how malaria is transmitted Reading 2: an informative piece on the social and political impact of malaria **Writing Activity:** An informative essay about a disease that interests you
Avoid plagiarism in all of your writing.	"Boston University Plagiarism" A university dean is asked to resign after using someone else's words in a speech.	Quotations in research	Reading 1: a definition of a research paper Reading 2: a sample research paper on the common cold **Writing Activity:** A research paper on the topic of your choice
Prepare for quizzes to help you in your classes.	"The Bush Family" A look at how this political family dealt with campaigning and made the adjustment to life in the spotlight.	Paragraph unity and coherence	Reading 1: a story about a conflict in philosophy between a father and his son Reading 2: a story about family traditions and conflicts **Writing Activity:** An analytical essay on the role of traditions in family life
Learn to work effectively in a group to help with group work assigned in all your classes.	"The Bilingual Education Controversy" A look at both sides of the controversial debate over bilingual education in the United States.	Eliminating wordiness	Reading 1: promotional material from a nonprofit organization asking for a donation Reading 2: an argument urging North Americans to examine their habit of moving frequently **Writing Activity:** A persuasive essay on what you believe is an important problem in your community
Consider your career options early to help you choose the right courses while you are in school.	"Summer Jobs" Advice on how to get a summer job.	Spelling rules	Reading 1: a research proposal for studying earthquakes written by a student **Writing Activity:** A proposal for a business or research project you would like to complete

Welcome to TAPESTRY!

Empower your students with the **Tapestry Writing** series!

Language learning can be seen as an ever-developing tapestry woven with many threads and colors. The elements of the tapestry are related to different language skills such as listening and speaking, reading, and writing; the characteristics of the teachers; the desires, needs, and backgrounds of the students; and the general second language development process. When all of these elements are working together harmoniously, the result is a colorful, continuously growing tapestry of language competence of which the student and the teacher can be proud.

Tapestry is built upon a framework of concepts that helps students become proficient in English and prepared for the academic and social challenges in college and beyond. The following principles underlie the instruction provided in all of the components of the **Tapestry** program:

- ◈ Empowering students to be responsible for their learning
- ◈ Using Language Learning Strategies and Academic Power Strategies to enhance one's learning, both in and out of the classroom
- ◈ Offering motivating activities that recognize a variety of learning styles
- ◈ Providing authentic and meaningful input to heighten learning and communication
- ◈ Learning to understand and value different cultures
- ◈ Integrating language skills to increase communicative competence
- ◈ Providing goals and ongoing self-assessment to monitor progress

Guide to **Tapestry Writing**

Setting Goals focuses students' attention on the learning they will do in each chapter.

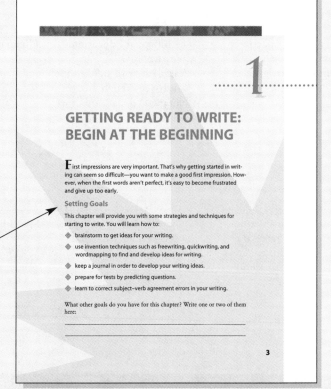

1

GETTING READY TO WRITE: BEGIN AT THE BEGINNING

First impressions are very important. That's why getting started in writing can seem so difficult—you want to make a good first impression. However, when the first words aren't perfect, it's easy to become frustrated and give up too early.

Setting Goals

This chapter will provide you with some strategies and techniques for starting to write. You will learn how to:

- ◈ brainstorm to get ideas for your writing.
- ◈ use invention techniques such as freewriting, quickwriting, and wordmapping to find and develop ideas for writing.
- ◈ keep a journal in order to develop your writing ideas.
- ◈ prepare for tests by predicting questions.
- ◈ learn to correct subject–verb agreement errors in your writing.

What other goals do you have for this chapter? Write one or two of them here:

3

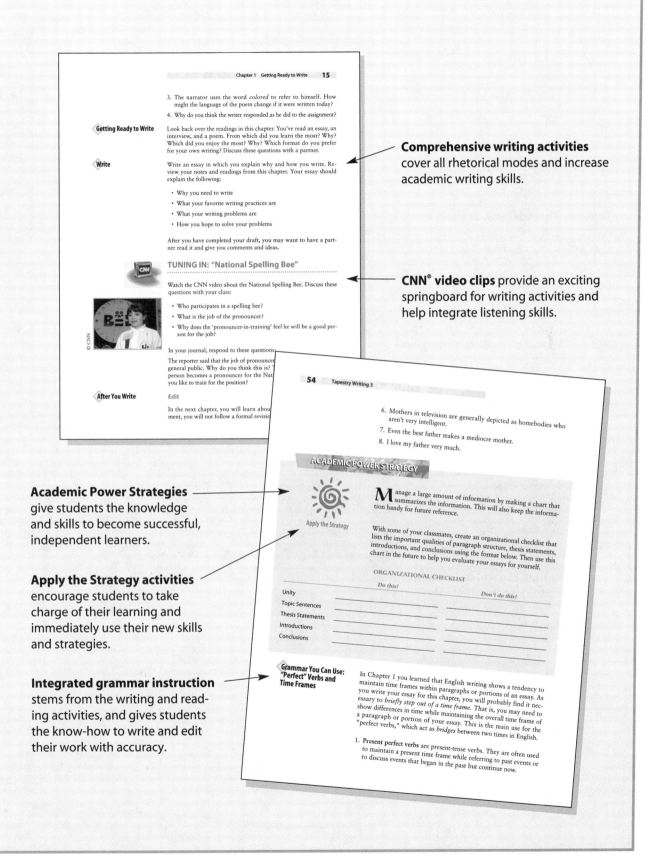

3. The narrator uses the word *colored* to refer to himself. How might the language of the poem change if it were written today?

4. Why do you think the writer responded as he did to the assignment?

Getting Ready to Write

Look back over the readings in this chapter. You've read an essay, an interview, and a poem. From which did you learn the most? Why? Which did you enjoy the most? Why? Which format do you prefer for your own writing? Discuss these questions with a partner.

Write

Write an essay in which you explain why and how you write. Review your notes and readings from this chapter. Your essay should explain the following:

• Why you need to write

• What your favorite writing practices are

• What your writing problems are

• How you hope to solve your problems

After you have completed your draft, you may want to have a partner read it and give you comments and ideas.

TUNING IN: "National Spelling Bee"

Watch the CNN video about the National Spelling Bee. Discuss these questions with your class:

• Who participates in a spelling bee?

• What is the job of the pronouncer?

• Why does the 'pronouncer-in-training' feel he will be a good person for the job?

In your journal, respond to these questions:

The reporter said that the job of pronouncer ... general public. Why do you think this is? ... person becomes a pronouncer for the Nat... you like to train for the position?

After You Write

Edit

In the next chapter, you will learn about ... ment, you will not follow a formal revisio...

Comprehensive writing activities cover all rhetorical modes and increase academic writing skills.

CNN® video clips provide an exciting springboard for writing activities and help integrate listening skills.

---

6. Mothers in television are generally depicted as homebodies who aren't very intelligent.

7. Even the best father makes a mediocre mother.

8. I love my father very much.

ACADEMIC POWER STRATEGY

Apply the Strategy

Manage a large amount of information by making a chart that summarizes the information. This will also keep the information handy for future reference.

With some of your classmates, create an organizational checklist that lists the important qualities of paragraph structure, thesis statements, introductions, and conclusions using the format below. Then use this chart in the future to help you evaluate your essays for yourself.

ORGANIZATIONAL CHECKLIST

	Do this!	Don't do this!
Unity		
Topic Sentences		
Thesis Statements		
Introductions		
Conclusions		

Grammar You Can Use: "Perfect" Verbs and Time Frames

In Chapter 1 you learned that English writing shows a tendency to maintain time frames within paragraphs or portions of an essay. As you write your essay for this chapter, you will probably find it necessary to *briefly step out of a time frame*. That is, you may need to show differences in time while maintaining the overall time frame of a paragraph or portion of your essay. This is the main use for the "perfect verbs," which act as *bridges* between two times in English.

1. **Present perfect verbs** are present-tense verbs. They are often used to maintain a present time frame while referring to past events or to discuss events that began in the past but continue now.

Academic Power Strategies give students the knowledge and skills to become successful, independent learners.

Apply the Strategy activities encourage students to take charge of their learning and immediately use their new skills and strategies.

Integrated grammar instruction stems from the writing and reading activities, and gives students the know-how to write and edit their work with accuracy.

Tapestry Threads provide students with interesting facts and quotes that jumpstart classroom discussions.

Stimulating reading selections model writing and grammar usage, and prepare students for the pre-writing, writing, and revising activities.

Language Learning Strategies help students maximize their learning and become proficient in English.

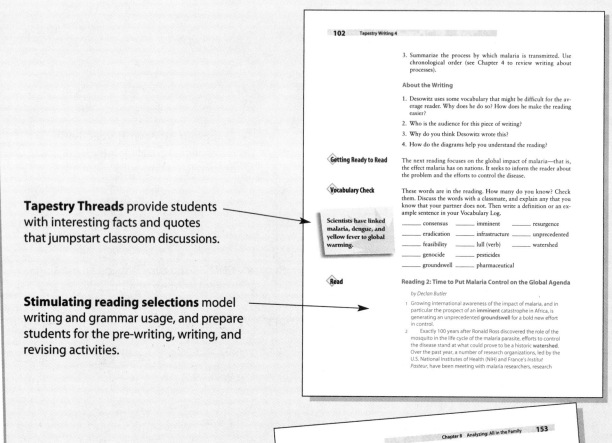

3. Summarize the process by which malaria is transmitted. Use chronological order (see Chapter 4 to review writing about processes).

About the Writing

1. Desowitz uses some vocabulary that might be difficult for the average reader. Why does he do so? How does he make the reading easier?

2. Who is the audience for this piece of writing?

3. Why do you think Desowitz wrote this?

4. How do the diagrams help you understand the reading?

Getting Ready to Read

The next reading focuses on the global impact of malaria—that is, the effect malaria has on nations. It seeks to inform the reader about the problem and the efforts to control the disease.

Vocabulary Check

These words are in the reading. How many do you know? Check them. Discuss the words with a classmate, and explain any that you know that your partner does not. Then write a definition or an example sentence in your Vocabulary Log.

> Scientists have linked malaria, dengue, and yellow fever to global warming.

____ consensus   ____ imminent   ____ resurgence

____ eradication   ____ infrastructure   ____ unprecedented

____ feasibility   ____ lull (verb)   ____ watershed

____ genocide   ____ pesticides

____ groundswell   ____ pharmaceutical

Read

Reading 2: Time to Put Malaria Control on the Global Agenda

by Declan Butler

1 Growing international awareness of the impact of malaria, and in particular the prospect of an **imminent** catastrophe in Africa, is generating an unprecedented **groundswell** for a bold new effort in control.

2 Exactly 100 years after Ronald Ross discovered the role of the mosquito in the life cycle of the malaria parasite, efforts to control the disease stand at what could prove to be a historic **watershed**. Over the past year, a number of research organizations, led by the U.S. National Institutes of Health (NIH) and France's *Institut Pasteur*, have been meeting with malaria researchers, research

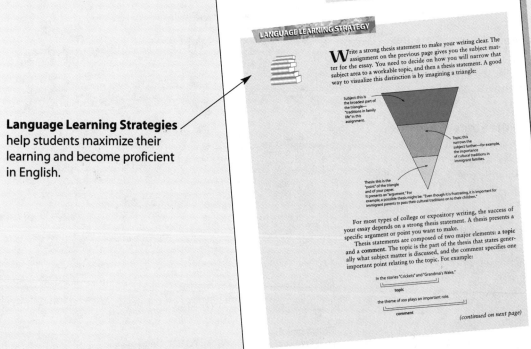

LANGUAGE LEARNING STRATEGY

Write a strong thesis statement to make your writing clear. The assignment on the previous page gives you the subject matter for the essay. You need to decide on how you will narrow that subject area to a workable topic, and then a thesis statement. A good way to visualize this distinction is by imagining a triangle:

Subject: this is the broadest part of the triangle—"traditions in family life" in this assignment.

Topic: this narrows the subject further—for example, the importance of cultural traditions in immigrant families.

Thesis: this is the "point" of the triangle and of your paper. It presents an "argument." For example, a possible thesis might be: "Even though it is frustrating, it is important for immigrant parents to pass their cultural traditions on to their children."

For most types of college or expository writing, the success of your essay depends on a strong thesis statement. A thesis presents a specific argument or point you want to make.

Thesis statements are composed of two major elements: a topic and a comment. The topic is the part of the thesis that states generally what subject matter is discussed, and the comment specifies one important point relating to the topic. For example:

In the stories "Crickets" and "Grandma's Wake,"
|_____|
       topic

the theme of xxx plays an important role.
|_____|
              comment

(continued on next page)

Test-Taking Tips offer students practical steps for improving their test results.

Check Your Progress helps students monitor their own progress.

Test-Taking Tip

Read essay questions carefully before beginning an essay test. As you think of ideas and examples you will want to include in your essay, jot these down on a piece of scrap paper or on the back of the test so that you can remember what you want to include in your essay. This will also help you to keep your mind clear of details and to focus on the larger ideas you want to communicate in your essay.

CHECK YOUR PROGRESS

On a scale of 1 to 5, rate how well you have mastered the goals set at the beginning of the chapter:

1 2 3 4 5   reflect on what you already know about a topic.

1 2 3 4 5   discover resources on campus and in your community to help you with research.

1 2 3 4 5   get and give feedback on writing.

1 2 3 4 5   avoid sentence fragments.

1 2 3 4 5   (your own goal) _____

1 2 3 4 5   (your own goal) _____

If you've given yourself a 3 or lower on any of these goals:

- visit the *Tapestry* web site for additional practice.
- ask your instructor for extra help.
- review the sections of the chapter that you found difficult.
- work with a partner or study group to further your progress.

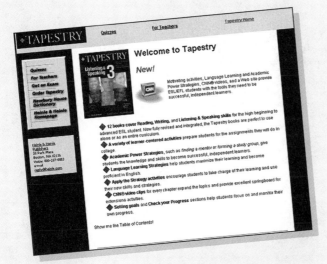

Expand your classroom at Tapestry Online
www.tapestry.heinle.com
- Online Quizzes
- Instructor's Manuals
- Opportunities to use and expand the Academic Power Strategies
- More!

For a well-integrated curriculum, try the **Tapestry Reading** series and the **Tapestry Listening & Speaking** series, also from Heinle & Heinle.

To learn more about the **Tapestry** principles, read *The Tapestry of Language Learning,* by Rebecca L. Oxford and Robin C. Scarcella, also from Heinle & Heinle Publishers. ISBN 0-8384-2359-0.

L ook closely at the photo, and then discuss these questions with your classmates:

- What types of writing do you enjoy doing?

- For whom do you like to write?

- Do you keep a journal? Why or why not?

GETTING READY TO WRITE: BEGIN AT THE BEGINNING

First impressions are very important. That's why getting started in writing can seem so difficult—you want to make a good first impression. However, when the first words aren't perfect, it's easy to become frustrated and give up too early.

Setting Goals

This chapter will provide you with some strategies and techniques for starting to write. You will learn how to:

◈ brainstorm to get ideas for your writing.

◈ use invention techniques such as freewriting, quickwriting, and wordmapping to find and develop ideas for writing.

◈ keep a journal in order to develop your writing ideas.

◈ prepare for tests by predicting questions.

◈ learn to correct subject–verb agreement errors in your writing.

What other goals do you have for this chapter? Write one or two of them here:

_____

_____

Getting Started

Discuss these questions with a partner or with your classmates:

- What is the most difficult part of starting the writing process for you?
- What do you think you do well when you write?
- What writing problem would you like more help with?

MEETING THE TOPIC

· ·

What are your writing practices? Have you ever thought about *how* you write? Do you write in a journal or at the computer? Do you write slowly, thinking over each word, or do you write in a frenzy and edit afterwards? In this chapter, you will think and write about your own practices, and learn how to improve upon them. You will also write about how and why people write.

Getting Ready to Read

LANGUAGE LEARNING STRATEGY

Brainstorm, or generate lists of ideas, to help you discover what you want to write about. **Brainstorming** means coming up with as many ideas as you can think of without stopping to think about or judge them. Brainstorming is an easy and popular technique for getting started in writing. You can brainstorm alone, with a partner, or with a group of classmates. You can brainstorm aloud, on paper, or in your head.

Brainstorming is what it sounds like—creating a "storm" of ideas in your head. Storms aren't slow, logical events that stop to think and correct themselves. They move quickly; you should, too.

Apply the Strategy

Brainstorm a list of all the reasons that you think learning to write well is important. If you are working alone, list all your ideas. If you're working in a group, keep talking and asking questions, writing them down as you discuss them. Here are two ideas to get you started:

- to do well on class papers
- to get a better job

Continue the list. Think of as many ideas as you can in five minutes. (If you are making one list as a group, be sure to make a copy of your list for everyone.)

Use invention techniques such as freewriting, quickwriting, and word mapping to find and develop ideas for writing. Freewriting, quickwriting, and word mapping are all techniques that writers use to discover ideas to write about. **Freewriting** means writing whatever comes to your mind, without being concerned with grammar or spelling. **Quickwriting** is similar to freewriting, but begins with a suggested, specific topic. All the other guidelines are the same as in freewriting: keep writing, and don't worry about spelling, punctuation, or grammar. Just continue to write and generate ideas. You can edit and revise later, if you want.

Word mapping is a way to link ideas together in a visual presentation. Take a piece of blank paper and write your topic in the center, then draw a circle or box around it. Next, write the main ideas of the topic in different places around it, and circle or box each of these. Draw arrows from your topic to each of those main ideas. Then work from each main idea and write some further ideas associated with those, continuing outward. An example is given for you in the following illustration:

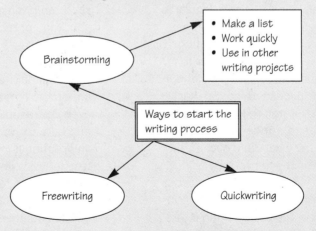

Apply the Strategy

Use the ideas you thought of in the brainstorming activity. Make a word map for the topic of why it's important to learn to write well.

In the following pages, you will read about these techniques and practice using them. The first technique you will read about is freewriting, a way to free the mind to find ideas without being limited by editing. This technique was developed by Peter Elbow, who explains this method in the following short essay.

◇ Vocabulary Check

The words and phrases in this list are taken from the following reading. How many of them do you know? Check them off. Look up the ones you don't, or discuss them with a classmate. Then write a definition or an example sentence in a Vocabulary Log. A Vocabulary Log is a notebook or section of a notebook used to record new words and phrases.

> Read, read, read.
> Read everything—
> trash, classics, good
> and bad, and see
> how they do it.
>
> **—WILLIAM FAULKNER**

_____ babbling

_____ catch-as-catch-can

_____ coherent

_____ compulsive

_____ garbled

_____ ingrained

_____ interpose

_____ jabbering

_____ magenta

_____ pertaining

_____ squiggle

_____ tactic

◇ Read

Reading 1: Freewriting

Peter Elbow

1   The most effective way I know to improve your writing is to do freewriting exercises regularly. At least three times a week. They are sometimes called "automatic writing," "**babbling**," or "**jabbering**" exercises. The idea is simply to write for ten minutes (later on, perhaps fifteen or twenty). Don't stop for anything. Go quickly without rushing. Never stop to look back, to cross something out, to wonder how to spell something, to wonder what word or thought to use, or to think about what you are doing. If you can't think of a word or a spelling, just use a **squiggle** or else write, "I can't think of it." Just put down something. The easiest thing is just to put down whatever is in your mind. If you get stuck it's fine to write "I can't think what to say, I can't think what to say" as many times as you want, or repeat the last word you wrote over and over again; or anything else. The only requirement is that you *never* stop.

2   What happens to a freewriting exercise is important. It must be a piece of writing which, even if someone reads it, doesn't send any ripples back to you. It is like writing something and putting it in a bottle in the sea. The teacherless[1] class helps your writing by providing maximum feedback. Freewritings help you by providing no feedback at all. When I assign one, I invite the writer to let me read it. But I also tell him to keep it if he prefers. I read it

---

[1]Peter Elbow wrote a book called *Writing Without Teachers*, a popular book about learning to write.

quickly and make no comments at all and I do not speak with him about it. The main thing is that a free writing must never be evaluated in any way; in fact there must be no discussion or comment at all.

3   Here is an example of a fairly **coherent** exercise (sometimes they are very incoherent, which is fine):

4   *I think I'll write what's on my mind, but the only thing on my mind right now is what to write for ten minutes. I've never done this before and I'm not prepared in any way—the sky is cloudy today, how's that? now I'm afraid I won't be able to think of what to write when I get to the end of the sentence—well, here I am at the end of the sentence—here I am again, again, again, again, at least I'm still writing—Now I ask is there some reason to be happy that I'm still writing—ah yes! Here comes the question again—What am I getting out of this? What point is there in it? It's almost obscene to always ask it but I seem to question everything that way and I was gonna say something else **pertaining** to that but I got so busy writing down the first part that I forgot what I was leading into. This is kind of fun oh don't stop writing—cars and trucks speeding by somewhere out the window, pens clittering across people's papers. The sky is cloudy—is it symbolic that I should be mentioning it? Huh? I dunno. Maybe I should try colors, blue, red, dirty words—wait a minute—no can't do that, orange, yellow, arm tired, green pink violent **magenta** lavender red brown black green—now that I can't think of any more colors—just about done—relief? maybe.*

5   Freewriting may seem crazy but actually it makes simple sense. Think of the difference between speaking and writing. Writing has the advantage of permitting more editing. But that's its downfall too. Almost everybody **interposes** a massive and complicated series of editings between the time words start to be born into consciousness and when they finally come off the end of the pencil or typewriter onto the page. This is partly because schooling makes us obsessed with the "mistakes" we make in writing. Many people are constantly thinking about spelling and grammar as they try to write. I am always thinking about the awkwardness, wordiness, and general mushiness of my natural verbal product as I try to write down words.

6   But it's not just "mistakes" or "bad writing" we edit as we write. We also edit unacceptable thoughts and feelings, as we do in speaking. In writing there is more time to do it so the editing is heavier: when speaking, there's someone right there waiting for a reply and he'll get bored or think we're crazy if we don't come out with *something*. Most of the time in speaking, we settle for the **catch-as-catch-can** way in which the words tumble out. In writing, however, there's a chance to try to get them right. But the opportunity to get them right is a terrible burden: you can work for two hours trying to get a paragraph "right" and discover it's not right at all. And then give up.

7   Editing, *in itself*, is not the problem. Editing is usually necessary if we want to end up with something satisfactory. The problem is that editing goes on *at the same time* as producing. The editor is, as it were, constantly looking over the shoulder of the producer and constantly fiddling with what he's doing while he's in the middle of trying to do it. No wonder the producer gets nervous, jumpy, inhibited, and finally can't be coherent. It's an unnecessary burden to try to think of words and also worry at the same time whether they're the right words.

8   The main thing about freewriting is that it is *nonediting*. It is an exercise in bringing together the process of producing words and putting them down on the page. Practiced regularly, it undoes the **ingrained** habit of editing at the same time you are trying to produce. It will make writing less blocked because words will come more easily. You will use up more paper, but chew up fewer pencils.

9   Next time you write, notice how often you stop yourself from writing down something you were going to write down. Or else cross it

out after it's written. "Naturally," you say, "it wasn't any good." But think for a moment about the occasions when you spoke well. Seldom was it because you first got the beginning just right. Usually it was a matter of a halting or even **garbled** beginning, but you kept going and your speech finally became coherent and even powerful. There is a lesson here for writing: trying to get the beginning just right is a formula for failure—and probably a secret **tactic** to make yourself give up writing. Make some words, whatever they are, and then grab hold of that line and reel in as hard as you can. Afterwards you can throw away lousy beginnings and make new ones. This is the quickest way to get into good writing.

10   The habit of **compulsive**, premature editing doesn't just make writing hard. It also makes writing dead. Your voice is damped out by all the interruptions, changes, and hesitations between the consciousness and the page. In your natural way of producing words there is a sound, a texture, a rhythm— a voice—which is the main source of power in your writing. I don't know how it works, but this voice is the force that will make a reader listen to you, the energy that drives the meanings through his thick skull. Maybe you don't *like* your voice; maybe people have made fun of it. But it's the only voice you've got. It's your only source of power. You better get back into it, no matter what you think of it. If you keep writing in it, it may change into something you like better. But if you abandon it, you'll likely never have a voice and never be heard.

11   Freewritings are vacuums. Gradually you will begin to carry over into your regular writing some of the voice, force, and connectedness that creep into those vacuums.

◆ After You Read

About the Content

1. Why is freewriting an important technique, according to Elbow?

2. Do you agree with Elbow that freewriting makes "simple sense"? What is your opinion of not getting feedback (teacher response) on your writing? Why do you think Elbow recommends no feedback on freewriting?

3. What are both the problems and advantages associated with editing?

4. What does Elbow mean by "nonediting" and "premature editing"? How can you avoid these problems?

5. What is a "voice" in writing?

About the Writing

1. How would you describe Elbow's "voice" in this essay? What type of style does he use to convey his message?

2. Elbow uses the second-person "you" in this writing. What effect does it have on the reader?

3. Locate a sentence or two in this essay that you think is well written. What is appealing about the sentence to you? Try to be specific.

Using the Strategies

- **Try freewriting:** Use Elbow's instructions, and freewrite *without stopping* for ten minutes about any topic you want.

- **Try quickwriting:** Think about an early experience you had with writing in English. What was it like for you? Try to recall that experience and quickwrite about it for 10 minutes. Remember, don't worry about spelling or grammar; just write as much as you can.

- **Try word mapping:** Create a word map using the word *music* as the starting box. Feel free to associate any other ideas you want; they don't have to be simple facts or information. Your feelings, reactions, and memories are part of the map.

You've now experimented with several invention techniques. Discuss the following questions:

1. Which invention strategy worked best for you? Why?

2. Which was the least effective? Explain your answer.

3. Do you have your own invention technique that wasn't described in this chapter? Explain your technique to your classmates.

> Anaïs Nin published diaries that she had written from age 11 until age 73. In one journal, she wrote, "We write to create a world in which we can live, to heighten our awareness of life, to lure and enchant and console others, to serenade our loves . . . and to transcend our life."

Getting Ready to Read

In the following interview, Lois Rosenthal talks to writer May Sarton about Sarton's journals. Before you read, find someone in your class who keeps a journal. Interview that person (or agree to be interviewed if you keep a journal). Some questions you might include in the interview are:

- How long have you kept your journal?

- How often do you write in it?

- Do you enjoy rereading things you wrote?

- What kinds of things do you write about in your journal?

- Do you ever let anyone read your journal?

Vocabulary Check

The words in this list are taken from the reading. Check off those that you know. Look up the ones you don't, or discuss them with a classmate. Then write a definition or an example sentence in your Vocabulary Log.

_____ daffodils	_____ lilac	_____ revel
_____ deluge	_____ nestled	_____ sampler
_____ distilled	_____ propel	_____ stupendous
_____ irises	_____ radiance	

Read

Reading 2: May Sarton

Lois Rosenthal

1 This passage—the entry for one entire day in _Journal of a Solitude_—is an excellent example of the way May Sarton looks at life:

2 _A gray day. . . but strangely enough, a gray day makes the bunches of **daffodils** in the house have a particular **radiance**, a kind of white light. From my bed this morning I could look through at a bunch in the big room, in that old Dutch blue-and-white drug jar, and they glowed. I went out before seven in my pajamas, because it looked like rain, and picked a **sampler** of twenty-five different varieties. It was worth getting up early, because the first thing I saw was a scarlet tanager[1] a few feet away on a **lilac** bush—**stupendous** sight! There is no scarlet so vivid, no black so black._

3 The mystical quality Sarton gives to what she sees around her moves readers of her journals to **deluge** her with letters telling her how much they identify with her feelings. As Sarton stops to **revel** in the beauty of a sunrise, as she is comforted by the warmth of a cat **nestled** next to her in bed during a worrisome night, she is able to **propel** these feelings straight to the heart of people who read her work. Then readers see their worlds as May Sarton sees hers—as poetry.

4 [May Sarton says], "Keeping a journal is much harder than it looks. I know that I have underrated its form compared to the novel and poetry and even the memoir, which is **distilled**, but there's no doubt it does have a discipline of its own. For any writer who wants to keep a journal, remember to be alive to everything, not just to what you're feeling, but also to your pets, to flowers, to what you are reading.

5 "Remember to write about what you are seeing every day, and if you are going to hold the reader's interest, you must write very well. And what does writing well mean? It means seeing very well, seeing in a totally original way.

[1]**scarlet tanager:** a type of red and black bird.

6   "Look at the bowl of **irises** on the table in front of me. Five different people who are asked to draw them would produce five totally different works of art, which is good. In the same way, journal writers must be just as honest in what they see because it's freshness that matters. Keeping a journal is exciting because it gives a certain edge to the ordinary things in life.

7   "Let's use another example. Say you've burned something in a pot, and you are standing at the sink scrubbing it. What comes to your mind as you are doing this? What does it mean to you in a funny way? Are you angry because you burn pots all too often? You can rage against the fact that it seems to be women who are mostly having to scrub pots, or you can ask yourself why you are bothering about this pot anyway. Why not throw it away if you can afford to get another? Is there something wrong with you that you are so compulsive you must try to clean something that is really beyond repair?

8   "Keeping a journal helps you get in touch with your own feelings. I think that's why I started the first one. I was in a depression when I began *Journal of a Solitude;* I was in the middle of a very unhappy love affair, and writing was my way of handling things.

9   "But a writer must always be perfectly honest. That's the key to people wanting to read a journal and that ingredient always astonishes me. When I've written things I felt were awfully weird and that no one would agree with, those are the very things that have made people say, 'you know, that's just how I feel.'

10   "My advice to any writer is never think of the effect of what you are doing while you are doing it. Don't project to a possible audience while you are writing. Hold on to your idea and get it down, and then maybe there'll be an audience, and maybe there won't. But have the courage to write whatever your dream is for yourself."

◆After You Read

About the Content

1. Why does Sarton think that writing in a journal is much harder than one might think?

2. Why does Sarton think that journal writing is exciting?

3. Summarize Sarton's advice for journal writers. Which advice seems like good advice?

About the Writing

Since this reading comes from an interview, rather than a written essay, what differences do you see between this and the Elbow essay?

FROM READING TO WRITING

Keep a journal in order to develop your writing ideas. As you have just read, a journal can be a good place to keep your different writing "experiments." In a writer's journal, you can put down your thoughts on any subject matter, at any time. You can be creative, analytical, even angry if you want to be. A writer's journal is another tool to help you develop ideas that you can later turn into polished pieces of writing. A journal can be kept in a notebook, on your computer, or in any form you want.

Apply the Strategy

Begin a journal for your writing class, in which you include responses to your readings. For your first entry, take Sarton's advice: write what you see right now. Look around the room and write about it in meaningful detail. Paint a picture with your writing.

Responding to a reading in your journal not only helps you think about the ideas an author presents; it also helps you formulate ideas for your own writing. You can take different approaches to your response—for example, you can analyze a reading, or you can react to it. Here is a list of questions you *might* ask. (But don't write your response just by answering these questions. Use them as a starting point to write your reactions to the reading.)

Analyzing

- What was the author's main point? Was it proven? How?

- Was the author biased in her or his presentation? How do you know?

- Was the author well informed? What kind of evidence was provided?

Reacting

- Did you enjoy the reading? Why or why not?

- Were you confused by any part of the essay or story? Explain the source of your confusion.

- What did you learn? What would you still like to learn?

Getting Ready to Read

Discuss these questions with your classmates:

- Why do you write?

- Why does anyone write?

Read the following poem, which explains why one person, Langston Hughes, wrote.

Langston Hughes was born in Joplin, Missouri, in 1902. He wrote poetry, fiction, and drama, and wrote regularly for the *New York Post*. He was an important figure in the Harlem Renaissance, a period of artistic growth centered around Harlem, a primarily African American section of New York City.

Reading 3: Theme for English B

Langston Hughes

The instructor said,

   Go home and write
   a page tonight.
   And let that page come out of you—
   Then, it will be true.

I wonder if it's that simple?
I am twenty-two, colored, born in Winston-Salem.[1]
I went to school there, then Durham, then here
to this college on the hill above Harlem.[2]
I am the only colored student in my class.
The steps from the hill lead down into Harlem,
through a park, then I cross St. Nicholas,
Eighth Avenue, Seventh, and then I come to the Y,[3]
the Harlem Branch Y, where I take the elevator
up to my room, sit down, and write this page:

It's not easy to know what is true for you or me
at twenty-two, my age. But I guess I'm what
I feel and see and hear, Harlem, I hear you:
hear you, hear me—we two—you, me, talk on this page.
(I hear New York, too.) Me—who?
Well, I like to eat, sleep, drink, and be in love.
I like to work, read, learn, and understand life.

[1] Winston-Salem and Durham: cities in North Carolina.

[2] This refers to Columbia University, which is near Harlem.

[3] **The "Y":** the YMCA, an organization that offers inexpensive rooms, as well as exercise classes and other activities.

I like a pipe for a Christmas present,
or records—Bessie,[4] bop, or Bach.
I guess being colored doesn't make me *not* like
the same things other folks like who are other races.
So will my page be colored that I write?
Being me, it will not be white.
But it will be
a part of you, instructor.
You are white—
yet a part of me, as I am a part of you.
That's American.
Sometimes perhaps you don't want to be a part of me.
Nor do I often want to be a part of you.
But we are, that's true!
As I learn from you,
I guess you learn from me—
although you're older—and white—
and somewhat more free.

This is my page for English B.

◆ After You Read

About the Content

1. What are the assignment and the instructions the student has been given? Do you think this is a good assignment?

2. What does the instructor mean by the idea that the writing should "come out of you"? How would you respond to that assignment?

3. In the lines that say the student is part of the instructor, and the instructor part of the student, what is the student trying to say?

4. The narrator also says the teacher might learn from him as much as he learns from the teacher. How might this be so?

About the Writing

> **Writing comes more easily if you have something to say.**
>
> —SHOLEM ASCH

1. What are some of the *images* (descriptions of things you can see or feel—for example, the fact that the university is on the hill above Harlem) of this poem? Explain their importance to the poem's meaning.

2. Do you think Hughes is the narrator (that is, the student who is speaking) of the poem? Why or why not?

---

[4]**Bessie:** Bessie Smith (1894–1937) was an American blues singer, considered to be the greatest jazz singer of her time.

3. The narrator uses the word *colored* to refer to himself. How might the language of the poem change if it were written today?

4. Why do you think the writer responded as he did to the assignment?

◈Getting Ready to Write

Look back over the readings in this chapter. You've read an essay, an interview, and a poem. From which did you learn the most? Why? Which did you enjoy the most? Why? Which format do you prefer for your own writing? Discuss these questions with a partner.

◈Write

Write an essay in which you explain why and how you write. Review your notes and readings from this chapter. Your essay should explain the following:

• Why you need to write

• What your favorite writing practices are

• What your writing problems are

• How you hope to solve your problems

After you have completed your draft, you may want to have a partner read it and give you comments and ideas.

TUNING IN: "National Spelling Bee"

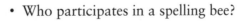

Watch the CNN video about the National Spelling Bee. Discuss these questions with your class:

• Who participates in a spelling bee?

• What is the job of the pronouncer?

• Why does the 'pronouncer-in-training' feel he will be a good person for the job?

© CNN

In your journal, respond to these questions:

The reporter said that the job of pronouncer goes unrecognized by the general public. Why do you think this is? Think about what kind of person becomes a pronouncer for the National Spelling Bee. Would you like to train for the position?

◈After You Write

Edit

In the next chapter, you will learn about revising. For this assignment, you will not follow a formal revision process. However, before you turn in your paper, you should make any changes you think will improve your paper. You can also give the paper to a classmate and get his or her suggestions.

Next, read the following information about subject–verb agreement, then edit your paper for subject–verb errors.

◇ Grammar You Can Use: Subject–Verb Agreement

A common problem among writers is not using correct subject–verb agreement. A basic rule of English grammar is that a singular subject takes a singular verb, and a plural or compound subject takes a plural verb. Unfortunately, it isn't always easy to determine the subject and whether or not it is plural. In addition, usage varies in spoken English, making the rules less certain.

The first thing you need to do is identify the true subject of a sentence. Sometimes the complete subject can be a whole phrase, but there is one word in that phrase that can be identified as the true subject. In the following example, the italicized phrase is the full subject phrase, but the underlined noun is the true subject:

> The <u>reason</u> that my dogs, ten German shepherds, bark so much is they are trained to listen for intruders.

That is, the full subject is *the reason that my dogs bark so much*, but the main subject is the word *reason*, which is singular, and takes the singular verb *is*. Don't be confused by long phrases that come between the subject and the verb.

However, even when you identify the main subject correctly, determining whether it is singular or plural can be confusing. The following chart lists ten common sources of confusion.

Subject Word	Number	Example
each, every, everybody, everyone	singular	*Each of the students <u>is</u> expected to attend.*
who, which, that, what	singular if the word it refers to is singular, plural if it is plural	a. *Who <u>is</u> going with me tonight?* b. *What <u>are</u> your ten favorite books?*
enough, none	singular if the word it refers to is singular, plural if it is plural	a. *Enough <u>are</u> present at the rally to make an impact.* b. *Enough <u>is</u> enough.*
there	When used as a subject, the verb agrees with the noun that comes after it.	a. *There <u>is</u> no reason to panic.* b. *There <u>are</u> no eggs in the refrigerator.*
either . . . or neither . . . nor	The verb agrees with the noun closest to it.	a. *Either that man or those women <u>have</u> the class notes.* b. *Neither the dogs nor the cat <u>is</u> making all that noise.*

Subject Word	Number	Example
expression of a unitary quantity before a plural	singular	a. *Twenty-six miles is a long way to run.* b. *Forty-five dollars is too expensive.*
a quantifier (*lot, much, many*) with *of*	singular if the noun that follows *of* is singular, plural if it is plural	a. *A lot of the men here are tall.* b. *Much of the book is hard to understand.*
the number of **a** number of	singular plural	a. *The number of students here today is ten.* b. *A number of students are going to the museum.*
names of countries, companies, institutions, areas of study ending in *-s*, and the word *news*	singular	a. *The Philippines was an important location during the war.* b. *The United Nations is an increasingly influential organization.* c. *Physics is my favorite class this term.* d. *The news is on at 11:00.*
titles	singular	*"Heroes" is my favorite song.*

Identify Subjects and Verbs

In the sentences below, identify the subjects and verbs. Underline the main subject, and double underline the verb that it goes with. The first is done for you as an example.

1. The dogs at the pet store are really cute.
2. Bob and his brothers are eating dinner with me tonight.
3. Each of the books is on my shelf.
4. Enough are present in class to begin the test.
5. What are your ten favorite books?

Now supply a present-tense verb that agrees with the subject in these sentences. Different answers may be possible.

6. A lot of the buildings in New York _____ really tall.
7. A number of cars _____ parked at the museum.
8. Either that girl or those boys _____ the new toy.
9. Four hundred dollars _____ too much to pay for that coat.
10. Much of the homework _____ difficult to do.
11. Neither those cars nor that bike _____ parked next to the fire hydrant.

12. One hundred kilometers _____ too far to drive so late.

13. The number of children here today _____ ten.

14. There _____ no reason to get up at 6:30 on Saturday.

15. There _____ only a few cars in the parking lot this morning.

Look at the sample student paragraph below, written about the poem "The Road Not Taken" by Robert Frost. Find the subject–verb agreement errors. Then rewrite the paragraph correctly.

Everyone is a traveler, choosing the roads to follow in their journey of life. There is never a direct path that give one only a single direction to follow. Regardless of the message that Robert Frost wanted to communicate, his poem "The Road Not Taken" have left its readers with many different interpretations. Readers' past, present and the attitude with which they see their futures determines how they understand the poem. However, this poem clearly demonstrate Frost's belief that it is the road that people chooses that make them who they are.

_____

_____

_____

_____

_____

Now check the subjects and verbs in your paper. Make sure that you have made no errors. Underline the subject of every sentence in your paper. Then find the verb. Correct any errors before you turn in the final paper.

> Writing is easy; all you do is sit staring at a blank sheet of paper until the drops of blood form on your forehead.
>
> —GENE FOWLER

PUTTING IT ALL TOGETHER

Use What You Have Learned

1. Brainstorm for 5 minutes on the following question: What strategies help you to get started writing? Write a list of ideas as you think of them.

2. Choose the strategy from this chapter that you think is most effective. Then quickwrite for 10 minutes about this strategy. Why do you think it's effective? How can it best be used? Remember, when you do a quickwrite, keep writing! Don't worry about grammar or spelling for now.

3. Edit your quickwrite for subject–verb agreement errors. Underline the subject of each sentence, and double underline the verbs. List

any errors you found on a separate piece of paper, and show the corrected form. Check your spelling, too.

Test-Taking Tip

One way to prepare for tests is to predict what will be on them. Try to predict the kinds of questions you would expect to find on the test. For example, imagine your teacher told you that you would be tested on the contents of this chapter. Write three questions you think might be on such a test. Be sure you review this chapter and your notes before you write your test questions. After you have written your questions, compare yours with those written by other classmates. Combine your questions, and you will have an excellent study guide for your next test.

CHECK YOUR PROGRESS

On a scale of 1 to 5, where 1 means "not at all," 2 means "not very well," 3 means "moderately well," 4 means "well," and 5 means "very well," rate how well you have mastered the goals set at the beginning of the chapter:

1 2 3 4 5   brainstorm to get ideas for your writing.

1 2 3 4 5   use invention techniques such as freewriting, quick-writing, and word mapping to find and develop ideas for writing.

1 2 3 4 5   keep a journal in order to develop your writing ideas.

1 2 3 4 5   prepare for tests by predicting questions.

1 2 3 4 5   learn to correct subject–verb agreement errors in your writing.

1 2 3 4 5   (your own goal) _____

1 2 3 4 5   (your own goal) _____

If you've given yourself a 3 or lower on any of these goals:

- visit the *Tapestry* web site for additional practice.
- ask your instructor for extra help.
- review the sections of the chapter that you found difficult.
- work with a partner or study group to further your progress.

ook closely at the photo, and then discuss these questions with your classmates:

- What is the story in this photo?
- Do you know a fascinating person?
- Do you like to read about people's lives?

2

NARRATION: A STORY TO TELL

Many writers enjoy telling stories—of their own lives or the lives of others. In this chapter, you will learn some of the techniques of writing stories, or narratives, about others and about yourself.

Setting Goals

This chapter will provide you with some strategies and techniques for writing interesting stories, or narratives. To write good stories, you will learn how to:

◈ reflect on what you already know about a topic.

◈ discover resources on campus and in your community to help you with research.

◈ get and give feedback on writing.

◈ avoid sentence fragments.

What other goals do you have for this chapter? Write one or two of them here.

_____

_____

Getting Started

Brainstorm (see page 4) a list of public figures (that is, people who are in the news or the media) that you think have had interesting lives. Don't worry about their stories yet; just write a list.

When you have finished, discuss your list with a partner. Choose the one person you think is the most interesting from the list.

MEETING THE TOPIC

Biographies are written to tell us important information and ideas about others' lives. In this section, you will write a simple biography of someone you admire. Read the following biography about Albert Einstein to see one example of how to write about a person's life.

Getting Ready to Read

What do you know about Albert Einstein? Discuss everything you already know with your class.

Vocabulary Check

The words in this list are included in the reading. How many of them do you know? Check the ones that you know and look up the ones you don't, or discuss them with a classmate. Then write a definition or an example sentence in your Vocabulary Log.

_____ amateur	_____ hypothesis
_____ anti-Semitism	_____ molecule
_____ astronomical	_____ patent
_____ authoritarianism	_____ renounce
_____ dyslexic	_____ speculate
_____ eclipse	_____ validation
_____ electromagnetism	_____ velocity
_____ headmaster	

Read

Reading 1: Albert Einstein (1879–1955), Physicist

1 Einstein was born in Ulm, Germany, and grew up in Munich[1], in a family of independent-minded, nonpracticing Jews. Little is known about his childhood. Because he was slow in learning to speak—he was not fully fluent even at the age of nine—he was at various times thought to be mentally retarded. Some experts have **speculated** that he was **dyslexic**. A **headmaster** once

[1]**Munich:** a city in Germany.

4   After graduating, he held several teaching jobs and became a technical assistant in the Swiss **Patent** Office in Bern, where he remained for six years. The job's great advantage, he later said, was that it gave him time to think about physics.

5   Between 1901 and 1904, Einstein published five papers on physics. In one paper he virtually proved the existence of **molecules**, solely by the use of theory; in another, he showed that light is both a wave and a particle. In his sixth paper, "On the Electrodynamics of Moving Bodies," published in the summer of 1905, he established the outline of his special theory of relativity. His arguments radically revised existing concepts of **electromagnetism**, light, and the behavior of moving bodies as set forth in Newtonian[3] physics. Einstein contended that the speed of light is constant and that nothing in the universe can travel faster than light. If the velocity of light is constant, then all motion and even time itself must be relative to it. If objects could approach the speed of light, their age, mass, and size would appear very different to a stationary observer than if the objects were moving at slower speeds. A clock nearing the speed of light would slow down; if it reached the speed of light, time would stand still. Many of his contentions have been confirmed by subsequent experiments. Atomic clocks in spacecraft orbiting the earth, for example, run a fraction of a second more slowly than clocks on earth.

told his father that what Einstein chose as a profession wouldn't matter, because "he'll never be a success at anything." At six he began learning to play the violin and became a gifted **amateur** violinist, maintaining this skill throughout his life.

2   Einstein attended the Luitpold Gymnasium[2] in Munich, which he disliked intensely for its **authoritarianism**. He was deeply interested in physics and mathematics and read eagerly in both subjects. Ultimately he rebelled, leaving Luitpold at fifteen without receiving his diploma.

3   Without a gymnasium diploma, Einstein could not enter a German university, so he enrolled in the Swiss Federal Polytechnic School in Zurich. He was so impressed with the democratic atmosphere of Switzerland that he formally **renounced** his German citizenship at the age of sixteen; in 1901 he was granted Swiss citizenship, which he retained for the rest of his life.

6   In the fall of 1905, Einstein published another short paper in which he proposed the famous equation $E = mc^2$: the energy in matter is equal to its mass multiplied by the square of the **velocity** of light. This equation explained how stars, like our own sun, can emit large amounts of light while losing very little mass, and it anticipated the splitting of the atom and the construction of the atom bomb 35 years later.

---

[2]**Gymnasium:** similar to high school in the United States.

[3]**Newtonian:** associated with Sir Isaac Newton, the scientist responsible for theories about the physical laws of the universe.

7   After receiving his doctorate from the University of Zurich in 1905, Einstein taught there and elsewhere until 1913, when he accepted a professorship in Berlin. There he established an Institute of Physics. He took up the question of gravity in his next major publication in 1916, "The Foundations of the General Theory of Relativity." One expert called it "the greatest feat of human thinking about nature." Whereas Newton had seen gravity as a universally present force, Einstein described it as a characteristic of matter. He proposed that gravity affected light just as it did matter and outlined both new structural laws and new laws of motion. The **validation** of the general theory was provided in 1919 by two English **astronomical** expeditions mounted to test its **hypothesis** by photographing an **eclipse** of the sun. When word was received that their results were positive, Einstein became the most famous scientist in the world overnight.

8   During the twenties, Einstein became more identified with his Jewish roots and worked to prevent another world war. In 1933, troubled by the swelling tide of **anti-Semitism** in Germany, he accepted an invitation to the Institute for Advanced Studies at Princeton, New Jersey,[4] where he remained for the rest of his life.

9   Einstein's scientific work from this point was devoted to his effort to create a unified field theory, linking electromagnetism and light. Although such a theory eluded him and other scientists proclaimed it impossible, he persisted with characteristic stubbornness. He consulted for the navy on the Manhattan Project during World War II, an action that went against his pacifist grain but seemed essential at the time because of the war's menace.

◆ After You Read

About the Content

1. What was Einstein like as a child?

2. Why did Einstein leave school?

3. Why did Einstein go to Switzerland?

4. What theory is Einstein most famous for?

5. What does "pacifist grain" mean in the last paragraph?

6. Where did Einstein spend the last part of his life?

About the Writing

1. What type of information about Einstein's life does this biography give?

2. What type of information does it leave out? What effect does that have on the writing, in your opinion?

3. What "style" would you say this writing is? Formal? Informal? Academic? Personal? Why do you think so?

4. How is this biography organized?

[4]**New Jersey:** a state on the east coast of the United States.

◀ **Getting Ready to Read**

Here is a different kind of biography, written in a different style. As you read this passage, think about the story and the language. Think also about the author's purpose in writing this passage.

◀ **Vocabulary Check**

The words in this list are included in the reading. Check those that you know. Look up the ones you don't, or discuss them with a classmate. Then write a definition or an example sentence in your Vocabulary Log.

_____ beneficent	_____ menial
_____ canny	_____ opulence
_____ contemplation	_____ pacemaker
_____ credo	_____ permeate
_____ destitute	_____ pestilential
_____ devout	_____ reproach
_____ hospice	_____ secular
_____ icon	_____ tuberculosis
_____ incessantly	_____ venerate
_____ indefatigable	_____ vocation
_____ leper	_____ whooping cough

> **If a nation loses its storytellers, it loses its childhood.**
>
> **—PETER HANDKE**

TUNING IN: "Mother Teresa"

Watch the CNN video about Mother Teresa. Discuss these questions with your class:

- What was remarkable about Mother Teresa's life?
- What kind of personality did she have?
- How did she influence the people around her?

In your journal, respond to this question:

- Many people say that "one person can't make a difference." Thinking about Mother Teresa's story, do you agree with that statement? In your journal, write about the difference you think one person can make.

© CNN

◆**Read**   **Reading 2:** Mother Teresa

1   Mother Teresa, who has died at age 87, stood out in an overwhelmingly **secular** age as a startling witness to the **beneficent** power of traditional religion.

2   The tiny nun in the cotton habit,[1] who founded in the slums of Calcutta an order[2] that grew into an international movement for the care of the sick, the dying, the outcast, proved that faith could indeed move mountains. Millions revered and **venerated** her as a saint.

3   At a time when most religious orders were shrinking, Mother Teresa's Missionaries of Charity expanded; today they operate more than 450 centers in over 100 countries. They feed 500,000 families a year; her schools teach 20,000 slum children; her clinics treat 90,000 **lepers**. More than 27,000 people, who might have died on the streets of Calcutta, have met a dignified end in her **hospices** for the dying.

4   Mother Teresa's mission was specifically to "the poorest of the poor" because she believed that the worst poverty of all was to reject a human soul in need. In 1985 she opened a hospice in New York for AIDS victims. "Don't you think they deserve our compassion?" she asked.

5   Statistics hardly convey her achievement. Those who visited the homes she established in the worst slums of Calcutta emerged overwhelmed by the love and cheerfulness that **permeated** the wards, bringing hope to the abandoned and dignity to the dying.

6   But the miracle was not achieved without intense physical effort. Mother Teresa confined herself to four hours sleep a night, rising at 4 a.m. from the floor of her tiny room to wash in a bucket before prayers.

7   Her frail body was welded to her immeasurably powerful soul with a meager diet of dhal[3] and rice. During the day she worked **incessantly** at the **menial** tasks that charity imposes; in the evenings, after administrative duties were done, she would address herself to hours of **contemplation** and prayer.

8   Through the decades, Mother Teresa's hard work and unceasing devotions gnarled her hands, lined her face and bent her back (she was only 4 ft 10 in. tall), creating the photographic **icon** that challenged the conscience of the world.

---

[1]**habit:** the name for nun's clothing, often a long black or white dress, and a type of hat, called a wimple.

[2]**an order:** a group of people living together under a religious rule.

[3]**dhal:** a type of Indian food.

9   It was part of Mother Teresa's **credo** that God would provide the means that her work demanded. She would forbid her helpers to raise money in her name. It made no difference: the funds flowed in.

10   Mother Teresa was **canny** as well as holy. At a press conference in Addis Ababa[4] in 1985, she innocently asked a government minister about an empty building she had seen on her way from the airport. In fact, she already knew all the details, and was able to embarrass the ignorant minister into turning it over to her purposes.

11   Mother Teresa's reputation secured the admiration of world leaders, religious and secular alike. Neither impressed by, nor dismissive of, their attention, she dealt with the mighty in the same friendly manner as she treated social outcasts.

12   Without resorting to charm, she knew how to get people to do what she wanted. Sometimes she did not trouble to hide her impatience at the ways of the world. "Why not put away your notebooks and do something useful?" she demanded of a group of journalists who had come to visit her.

13   It is the mark of the saint to attract hostility. In Calcutta there were some Hindus who, inclined to regard poverty as an unalterable part of the divine scheme, looked askance at Mother Teresa's efforts to relieve it, and concluded that she must be a CIA agent. To the Western liberal conscience it appeared as a particular **reproach** that Mother Teresa's works of charity stemmed from an unyieldingly conservative religious stance.

14   In 1990 Germaine Greer launched a full-blooded attack on Mother Teresa as a religious imperialist, who used her charity as a method of foisting Catholicism on vulnerable people. In fact, the Missionaries do not preach at those they assist; if they make converts, it is by exam-

ple. "I do convert," admitted Mother Teresa. "I convert you to be a better Hindu, a better Catholic, Muslim, Jain or Buddhist."

15   The youngest of three children, Gonxha ("Rosebud") Agnes Bojaxhiu was born on August 27, 1910, at Skopje, in a largely Muslim area of what is now Macedonia. She was a frail child, susceptible to malaria[5] and **whooping cough.**

16   Her father, a successful merchant in sympathy with Albanian patriots, died when she was eight. Her mother was a **devout** Catholic who instilled a special awareness of the needs of the poor: "When you do good," she instructed, "do it unobtrusively, as if you were tossing a pebble into the sea."

17   Agnes Bojaxhiu did outstandingly well at school and was an accomplished musician. But by the age of 12 she was already resolved to become a nun, and as a teenager she devoured Catholic magazines, being particularly struck by reports of Croatian and Slovene missionaries in Calcutta.

18   Though there were moments in adolescence when she doubted her **vocation**, at 18 she left home to enter the Order of Loreto in Ireland, a choice dictated by the fact that the nuns worked in India. There she adopted the religious name Sister Mary Teresa of the Child Jesus—after St. Therese, "the Little Flower," who in 1897, at the age of 24, had died of **tuberculosis** in a convent at Lisieux.

[4]**Addis Ababa:** a city in Ethiopia

[5]Read more about malaria in Chapter 6.

19   A year later, Sister Teresa was sent out to teach in the subcontinent. After a novitiate[6] in Darjeeling, she joined the Loreto convent in Calcutta. The convent had a school, St. Mary's, in its grounds, where she taught geography and history to well-off Bengali girls.

20   The convent was close to Calcutta's notorious Motijhil slum, and between classes Sister Teresa took medicine and clothing to the poor. But the contrast between her classroom and the slums did not at once convince her that she should devote her life to caring for the **destitute**.

21   She took her final vows in May 1937, and immediately—as "Mother Teresa"—became the headmistress of St. Mary's. But letters from her mother reinforced her growing conviction that her destiny lay elsewhere.

22   The moment of truth came on a train for Darjeeling, on September 10, 1946. She heard what she said was without doubt a call from God to serve the poorest of the poor. Being already a nun, she described the experience as "a call within a call."

23   Initially she had to overcome opposition from the Catholic establishment. Her request to be freed from the Loreto Order to devote her life to caring for the poor was shelved for two years. An archbishop remarked: "I knew this woman as a novice. She could not light a candle in the chapel properly—and you expect her to start a congregation?"

24   Nevertheless, early in 1948 the General Superior of the Loreto Order in Ireland gave her permission to found a new order, providing the venture was authorized by Rome. Pope Pius XII gave his blessing in April 1948, and ordained that the new order should be under direct obedience to the Archbishop of Calcutta. That August, Mother Teresa exchanged the habit of Loreto for a simple sari[7] and sandals.

25   A circular to all Loreto schools in Calcutta announced she had left her convent: "Do not speak about it. Do not criticize. Do not praise it. Pray."

26   Mother Teresa took a nurses' training course with the Medical Missionary Sisters at Patna, and then, though inclined to faint at the sight of blood, went out into the **pestilential** horrors of Calcutta. Conditions were especially bad at that time because of the refugees flooding in from east Bengal. Mother Teresa was already approaching 40. "Today, my God, what tortures of loneliness," she noted in her diary after one of these ventures.

27   Her first establishment was a small, open-air school in Motijhil, where she taught children to read and write. The first Sisters were her former pupils from St. Mary's. As the order's work became known, funds began to flow in from more distant sources. The money was devoted exclusively to the outcasts of society. "Being unwanted," Mother Teresa believed, "is the worst disease that any human being can ever experience."

28   The Sisters rescued new-born babies abandoned on rubbish heaps; they sought out the sick; they took in lepers, the unemployed, and the mentally ill.

29   Mother Teresa insisted that overheads at all homes instituted under her rule should not exceed two percent of total expenditure. Her example was matched by her followers. Each Sister had two sets of clothes, wearing one while she washed the other. Their food per head cost about four pounds a month: enough to nourish them through each 14-hour day.

30   The vow of poverty was more strict than in other orders because, in Mother Teresa's view, "to be able to love the poor and know the poor we must be poor ourselves." As Superior General she would become fretful at signs of **opulence**. "We cannot work for the rich," she

[6]**novitiate:** a period of time when one is a novice, or in training to become a nun.

[7]**a sari:** an Indian-style dress.

insisted, "neither can we accept any payment for what we do."

31   Mother Teresa took Indian citizenship in 1949. By 1950 there were seven nuns, and that year the congregation was officially recognized by Rome as the Society of the Missionaries of Charity.

32   In 1953, the community moved into the house that is still its headquarters: 54a Lower Circular Road. There they established the two types of homes as the models for all their subsequent work: Shishu Bhavan, a children's home, and Nirmal Hriday ("Place of the Pure Heart"), a home for dying destitutes, which had been a Kali temple hostel and was donated by the city of Calcutta.

33   Special treatment for lepers began in 1957. Three years later, it began to expand beyond Calcutta. Within a few years the Order was established in 23 cities.

34   During the 1960s, thanks to free tickets from Air India, Mother Teresa began to travel, establishing new houses all over the world—in Venezuela (1965), Tanzania (1968), and Australia (1969).

35   Some opposition was found in South America, particularly in Peru, where some churchmen were concerned that easing the hardships of the poor would weaken the opposition to repressive regimes.

36   By the 1980s Mother Teresa had become a familiar figure at scenes of disaster. During the Israeli invasion of Lebanon in 1982 she rescued half-starved children in Beirut. In 1986 she escaped unhurt when her light aircraft crashed on a rough airstrip in Tanzania, killing five spectators in the crowd waiting to greet her. The next year her work extended into the Vatican itself: the Pope gave her the task of supervising a hospice for down-and-outs within the City's walls.

37   Even Fidel Castro[8] allowed her to undertake a mission in Havana, and in 1987 the Soviet Union agreed that she could send nuns to work in a hospital.

38   In 1988 she visited London, which she called "the Cardboard City" on account of the number of people whom she found sleeping outdoors in boxes. She called Mrs. Thatcher "wonderful" after the Prime Minister had promised to set up a hostel for down-and-outs in central London. But a year later, Mother Teresa complained, no hostel had been provided.

39   Although she remained **indefatigable,** her health had long been giving cause for concern. She suffered a slight stroke in 1974 and a heart attack in 1983 while visiting the Pope. In 1989 doctors in Calcutta implanted a **pacemaker.** In April 1990 poor health forced her to announce her retirement as Superior of the Missionaries of Charity.

40   In the spring of 1991 she visited her native Albania, where she established a mission in Tirana. Her presence helped to reinvigorate religious life after a 23-year ban.

41   Ill health increased in her last years. But she remained alert enough to promise her prayers on the death of Diana, Princess of Wales: "She was extremely sympathetic to poor people—and very lively, and homely too."

42   Mother Teresa, who so sternly rejected the tinsel delights of this world, discovered that the world was determined to heap honors on her. Her awards included the Nehru Award for International Understanding in 1972, the first Albert Schweitzer International Prize in 1975, the Nobel Peace Prize in 1979, and an honorary Order of Merit presented by the Queen in Delhi in 1983.

43   Death held no terrors for Mother Teresa. "Heaven for me," she said, "will be the joy of being with Jesus and Mary and all other saints and angels, and all our poor—all of us going home to God."

44   As for the future, Mother Teresa said: "Just as God has found me, He will find somebody else."

[8]**Fidel Castro:** the president of Cuba.

After You Read

About the Content

1. What is meant by "a secular age"?

2. What type of people do Mother Teresa's convents serve?

3. What was Mother Teresa's daily life like?

4. What groups have objected to Mother Teresa's work? Why?

5. What was Mother Teresa's childhood like?

6. Why did she decide to devote her life to the poor and sick?

7. What is a "vow of poverty"? Why was it important to Mother Teresa?

About the Writing

1. What is the purpose of this reading passage?

2. How is the organization different from the passage about Einstein?

3. How is the style different from the passage about Einstein?

4. What is the author's *attitude* towards Mother Teresa? What individual words or phrases tell you that attitude? Underline those words or phrases and discuss why they're important to the passage.

From the list you created in your brainstorming session, choose one person you would like to write about. Then begin your research.

LANGUAGE LEARNING STRATEGY

Reflect on what you already know, and find out what others know about your topic to help you begin your writing. You can begin your research right in your classroom. Before you go to the library or on the Internet, you can learn a lot about the person you chose. Start by thinking about what you already know. You can make a list or do some preliminary writing. Then find out what your classmates know.

Apply the Strategy

Write the name of the person you will research at the top of a piece of paper. Write what you know about the person. Then put the paper on your desk or table. Walk around the room and look at everyone's papers. If you know something about another person selected, write it on his or her paper.

ACADEMIC POWER STRATEGY

Apply the Strategy

Discover the resources on campus and in your community for research. In order to complete this assignment, you will have to do some research about the person you chose to write about. How can you go about doing that? In all of your classes, it will help you to know where you can find information in your community.

Complete this checklist:

1. Where is the closest library? _____

   _____

2. What are its hours? _____

   _____

3. Is there another library you can use if you need to? _____

4. Where is it, and what are its hours? _____

   _____

   _____

5. Does the library have a video collection? _____

6. Where can you use the Internet for research? _____

   _____

7. What are the addresses of one or two Internet sites that will help you search for information? _____

   _____

FROM READING TO WRITING

• •

You have read two different kinds of biographies. One was a neutral account of Einstein's life. Its purpose was not to praise or condemn him, but merely to report the facts of his education and career. The story of Mother Teresa, which was an obituary, had a different purpose; it told not only the story of her life, but also praised her for her work with the poor.

For your essay, you will have to decide what kind of biography you will write and what organization you will use.

◀ Getting Ready to Write

Narrating a Story

It is likely that your subject might be too complicated to cover in a short essay. So, when you tell the story, you have choices to make in order to make the writing task more manageable. Think about these questions:

> There are only two or three human stories, and they go on repeating themselves as fiercely as if they had never happened before.
>
> —WILLA CATHER

- What will be your *position*? That is, what attitude do you hold towards your subject? You can be *neutral*, without a positive or negative opinion about your subject. You can also praise your subject, or talk about the good aspects of his or her life. You can also condemn the person for the life he or she has led. Of course, it is possible to mix negative and positive aspects of someone's life in your biography, too.

- How *much* of the story do you want to tell? It may be too difficult to tell the story of someone's entire life. It can be interesting to tell only about someone's childhood, or adult life, for example.

- What *topics* will you cover? Will you talk about both the person's personal and professional life, or only one?

- How will you *organize* the story? A common choice is *chronological*—that is, in the order in which events happened. However, there are other possibilities. For example, you might organize the story by *themes* or major ideas, or you might have another idea for the organization.

Gather your notes and ideas about the person whose biography you will write. Then complete the following chart in order to decide how you will write your essay.

1. What *position* will you take toward your subject? Explain your choice.

   - Neutral: A neutral position tells only the facts.

   - Positive: A positive position praises the person for his or her accomplishments.

   - Negative: A negative position condemns the person for the life he or she has led.

   My reasons: _____

   _____

   _____

2. What part (or events or incidents) of the person's life will you write about?

   From _____

   to _____

   Reasons: _____

   _____

   _____

3. What topics will you cover?

   Reasons: _____

   _____

   _____

4. How will you organize your essay?

   - chronologically

   - by theme or main ideas

   - other (explain):

   Reasons: _____

   _____

   _____

5. What other things are you thinking about for your essay?

   Notes: _____

   _____

   _____

You now have your notes and ideas for your essay. Look at one more sample of writing, this one done by a student:

Jules Verne

Jules Verne was a remarkable writer who predicted the world's scientific future. Some of the inventions he imagined were created later in his lifetime, but some still haven't been invented. He was a favorite of all kinds of readers: rich and poor, young and old, scientists and artists, and of course, average folks. He wrote over 80 books, mostly before 1900. A few of the things he depicted in his books were: helicopters, submarines, modern weapons, movies with sound, rockets, and even television.

Jules Gabriel Verne was born in 1828, in Nantes, France. Verne's parents came from families of sailors, a fact which had an important influence on his writing. When he was a boy, Jules Verne ran away from his family to become a ship's cabin boy, but he was caught and taken back to his parents. Then, in 1847 he traveled to Paris to study law. While he was there, he acquired a love for the theater and began to write plays. In 1850, Jules Verne's first play was published. His father was irate when he found out that Jules was not going to continue to study law, so he discontinued his allowance for his expenses. It was then that Verne decided to earn money by selling his stories.

Jules Verne spent a lot of his time in Parisian libraries studying geology, engineering, and astronomy. He connected his reading to his writing. He published his first novel, <u>Five Weeks in a Balloon</u>, in 1863. Soon he started writing many more novels. His most famous ones are: <u>Journey to the Center of the Earth</u> (1864), <u>From the Earth to the Moon</u> (1865), <u>Twenty Thousand Leagues Under the Sea</u> (1870), <u>Around the World in Eighty Days</u> (1873), and <u>The Mysterious Island</u> (1874). A few of his novels have been turned into movies, like <u>20,000 Leagues Under the Sea</u> and <u>Around the World in 80 Days</u>.

Jules Verne became a very rich man because of his writing. In 1876, he bought a large yacht and sailed around Europe. Afterwards, he wrote a lot about sailing.

Although Jules Verne died on March 24, 1905, he has maintained his reputation as the father of modern science fiction and the inventor of many imaginary things which, in time, have become realities.

For Class Discussion

1. How did this writer organize her ideas?

2. What attitude did she take toward her subject?

3. What topics did she cover?

4. How could this writing be improved?

Write

Peer Response

Tell a partner or a small group of classmates the main ideas of your story. After each group member tells his or her story, the group should interview the storyteller about his or her ideas. Here are a few questions you might ask, although you should add your own questions to this list:

- Why did you choose this person to write about?
- What is the most interesting thing about this person's life?
- What do you think will be difficult to write about?
- How do you want the reader to feel about this person?

> **Good writing is clear thinking made visible.**
>
> **—BILL WHEELER**

After all the stories are told and the group members interviewed, each person should take 5 to 10 minutes to write any new thoughts or ideas that might be added to his or her essay.

Drafting

You now have several pieces of writing and notes for your essay. Take an inventory (review of what you have) to see if you are ready to start writing your first draft. Answer the following questions about your preparation so far:

- Will I be able to supply enough details about the person?
- Do I know what attitude I want to take in my writing?
- Do I know how I am going to organize the story?
- Will my story be interesting to my audience?

If you aren't sure about any of these questions, use quickwriting or other techniques to fill in any gaps in your story.

When you are satisfied that you have gathered enough information to begin writing, you can write the draft of your essay.

◆ After You Write

Get and give feedback on writing to improve your writing and the writing of your classmates. Nearly all writers ask others to read their work critically. Having "another pair of eyes" look at your work can help you find problems you can't see. An outside reader can tell you things that are difficult to understand, or make suggestions about better use of language.

Apply the Strategy

Exchange your draft with a classmate, and read it carefully. Then use Part I of the following review chart to comment on your classmate's story. When your classmate returns your essay and his or her comments, respond to the review by completing the questions in Part II of the review sheet.

Writer's Name _____

Reviewer's Name _____

Part I. (to be written by the reviewer; please answer all questions completely and specifically)

Title of Essay _____

1. Is this an interesting and appropriate title? Explain.	
2. Recopy the first sentence of the essay. Is it intriguing? Boring? Explain. If you don't like it, how would you rewrite it?	
3. What *position* did the author take toward his or her subject? Is it clear? How could that position be made clearer?	
4. Find the most effective sentence in the essay and label it. What makes it effective?	
5. Find a weak sentence and label it. How could it be improved?	

6. Locate three words or phrases that should be made clearer. Circle them. Can you suggest better choices?	
7. What kind of organization did the author use? Were any of the details of the organization confusing?	
8. Are the details of the story clear? If anything is confusing, point it out.	
9. How does the essay end? What impression does it leave you with? If it needs improvement, explain what might improve it.	
10. What is your overall impression of the essay? What would you do to improve it?	

Part II. (to be written by the author of the essay)

1. Do you think you need to change your title? If so, how will you change it?	
2. Will you change the opening of your essay? If so, how?	
3. Do you agree that the sentence chosen as weak by your reviewer needs changing? If not, why not? If so, how will you change it?	
4. How will you make the three weak words better? Is it necessary?	
5. How will you improve the organization?	
6. Will you make any changes to the ending? Why or why not?	
7. Do you agree with your reviewer's overall comments about your paper?	

Revise

Revision is not merely correcting your spelling and grammar and inserting a few commas. In the revision phase of the writing process, you are reorganizing, cutting, adding details, and improving your choices. Looking at the review you received from your partner and your response to it, formulate a revision plan. Use the following chart to help you identify the areas that need the most improvement.

Feature	Problem	Possible Solution
Title		
Opening paragraph		
Story		
Organization		
Word choice		
Conclusion		
Other		

Use your revision plan to guide your rewriting.

Edit

After you have solved the problems identified in your revision plan, you can focus on editing and proofreading your paper. The editing phase includes double-checking your grammar, spelling, punctuation, and so forth. Each student has unique problems in this area, so it may be helpful to take an inventory of problem spots, based on your past experience as a writer. You can change this inventory as you progress.

Which of the following items do you think are a problem for you? Check the appropriate column.

PROBLEM	MAJOR PROBLEM	MINOR PROBLEM	NO PROBLEM	DON'T KNOW
Spelling	_____	_____	_____	_____
Punctuation	_____	_____	_____	_____
Subject–verb agreement	_____	_____	_____	_____
Verb tenses	_____	_____	_____	_____
Articles and prepositions	_____	_____	_____	_____
Plurals	_____	_____	_____	_____
Sentence fragments	_____	_____	_____	_____
Run-on sentences	_____	_____	_____	_____
Wordiness	_____	_____	_____	_____
Transitions	_____	_____	_____	_____
Relative clauses	_____	_____	_____	_____

If you have checked more than three as a "major problem," decide which three you would like to work on first. It's easier to concentrate on a few problem areas at a time.

The last step should be proofreading—that is, looking for careless mistakes: misspellings, leaving out words, typing words twice in a row, and so forth. Before you turn your paper in, proofread it carefully.

Grammar You Can Use: Sentence Fragments

Sentence fragments lack some word or phrase that is needed to make them full sentences. Look at the examples below. What's wrong with these sentences?

I met him on a train many years ago. Coming home from New York.
He was an amazing man. A man who had traveled all over Asia, and lived in many countries.

In both these examples, the first period should be replaced by a comma and the two sentences joined into one. That is because the second sentence is a fragment. Sometimes it is acceptable to stress a word or phrase in your writing:

I called her many times. No answer.

If you do this, however, be sure that the emphasis is necessary and that it is clear you have done this on purpose.

Look at the sentences below. Decide which of them are fragments; then decide if they need to be fixed. If they do, rewrite them correctly.

1. From a professional point of view, a good résumé is an invaluable tool, according to Dr. Thomas DiPietro. Who teaches business communication at the University of Manitoba.

2. Walking along the river, throwing stones into the clear green water, which looked so inviting that I wanted to jump in.

3. "There was an elder brother described by my father as: 'Too damned clever by half. One of those quick, clever brains. . . .'"
—Doris Lessing

4. "Can such principles be taught? Maybe not. But most of them can be learned."—William Zinsser

5. Most banks offer different types of mortgages. The fixed rate mortgage, which guarantees the same rate for the life of the loan, and the adjustable rate mortgage (ARM), which will fluctuate with changing interest rates.

Self-Correction

In a recent piece of writing, identify areas where you had difficulty with fragments. Copy any sentences with fragment errors in them; then rewrite each sentence correctly.

PUTTING IT ALL TOGETHER

In this chapter, you have learned to do simple research, to discover what you already know about a topic, to get and give feedback on your writing, and to avoid fragment sentences.

You have written about someone else's life for your assignment. Now choose one short period or event from your life that you would like to write about. Write for 15 minutes in your journal about this event in your life.

Test-Taking Tip

Read essay questions carefully before beginning an essay test. As you think of ideas and examples you will want to include in your essay, jot these down on a piece of scrap paper or on the back of the test so that you can remember what you want to include in your essay. This will also help you to keep your mind clear of details and to focus on the larger ideas you want to communicate in your essay.

CHECK YOUR PROGRESS

On a scale of 1 to 5, rate how well you have mastered the goals set at the beginning of the chapter:

1 2 3 4 5   reflect on what you already know about a topic.

1 2 3 4 5   discover resources on campus and in your community to help you with research.

1 2 3 4 5   get and give feedback on writing.

1 2 3 4 5   avoid sentence fragments.

1 2 3 4 5   (your own goal) _____

1 2 3 4 5   (your own goal) _____

If you've given yourself a 3 or lower on any of these goals:

- visit the *Tapestry* web site for additional practice.

- ask your instructor for extra help.

- review the sections of the chapter that you found difficult.

- work with a partner or study group to further your progress.

L ook at the photo, and then discuss these questions with your classmates:

- Do you know any famous architects' work?
- Do you enjoy going to museums?
- Who is your favorite artist?

3

DESCRIPTION: BUILDING IMAGES

Writers often write descriptions. Descriptions are useful for many types of writing: scientific, creative, and academic. Descriptions enable the reader to see, hear, and feel what is being written about. Good description engages all of the reader's senses. In this chapter, you will apply descriptions to the field of architecture.

Setting Goals

This chapter will provide you with some strategies and techniques for writing descriptions. You will learn how to:

◈ use pictures to help you visualize what you are going to write about.

◈ understand the specialized vocabulary of a field or profession.

◈ use dictionaries effectively.

◈ avoid and fix run-ons, comma splices, and misused conjunctions.

What other goals do you have for this chapter? Write one or two of them here:

_____

_____

Getting Started

Quickwrite

Look around the room you are in right now. Take 10 minutes and write a description of the room. Think about the shapes you see, the light, the main features, etc. Remember that in a quickwrite, you shouldn't worry about spelling and grammar. Just let the ideas flow. (See page 5 for a description of how to do quickwrites.)

MEETING THE TOPIC

In this chapter, you will learn to write effective descriptions, especially descriptions of buildings and artwork. As you work through this chapter, think about different ways to describe things, and how descriptions are used in writing.

Look at this photo. How would you describe this building? Discuss it with your classmates.

The Eiffel Tower was built for the International Exhibition of Paris of 1889 commemorating the 100th birthday of the French Revolution. Of the 700 proposals submitted in a design competition, Gustave Eiffel's was unanimously chosen.

Getting Ready to Read

In this reading, the author talks about the "secret homes" of children. Before you read, think about these questions: Did you have a secret place when you were a child? What was it like?

Vocabulary Check

The words and phrases in this list are included in the reading. Check those that you know. Look up the ones you don't, or discuss them with a classmate. Then write a definition or an example sentence in your Vocabulary Log.

_____ autonomy   _____ peekaboo

_____ gamekeeper   _____ perimeter

_____ hide-and-seek   _____ quarry

_____ homestead   _____ thatched

_____ nostalgic   _____ vantage point

_____ nurturance

 Read

Reading 1: Secret Homes

Clare Cooper Marcus

> Architecture, of all the arts, is the one which acts the most slowly, but the most surely, on the soul.
>
> **—ERNEST DIMNET**

1   As infants, we relate primarily to mother or other primary caregiver. We are dependent on this other being for food, care, **nurturance**, protection, and love. As we start to mature into early childhood, we begin to explore the space we occupy; we touch and throw and hit and crawl to discover the nature of the "stuff" around us. Gradually, and with greater assurance, we begin to explore the world outside the protection of home. First under the watchful eye of an adult, and then alone in a setting that adults may have created partially for our safe use (yard, garden, play area), we dig, break sticks, pick up leaves, watch insects, climb trees, and create river systems in the sandbox. We learn what the world outside is made of; we learn how we can manipulate it to satisfy our questioning minds, our sensing fingertips, our excitement-seeking emotions. We play at now-you-see-me-now-you-don't, at first through **peekaboo**, and then by running ahead in the park and bouncing out from behind a bush, then by playing **hide-and-seek** with our friends, and, finally, by creating a secret place (cubby,[1] clubhouse, den, hideout) which our parents may not ever know about.

2   Part of the process of growing up is learning to do without our parents, to move bit by bit away from their nurturance and watchful eyes, and to test ourselves in those parts of the environment that are "not home." We act out the inevitable process of separation via games and activities in the environment. One way in which children do this is to create their own homes-away-from-home, like **homesteads** on the frontier. Such place-making activities are almost universal in childhood, regardless of culture, social context, or gender. They are part of the process of growing up. For some people, that place of initial separation and **autonomy**, that secret home-away-from-home, lingers in adult life as a powerful and **nostalgic** memory.

[1]**cubby**: a small hiding place.

3   For myself, two places stand out among many secret settings we found or made. One was "The Hut," built by my brother and his friends out of poles and flattened-out army gasoline cans, in a wood near our house. It had a "**thatched**" roof of branches and leaves, a **perimeter** fence and gate, and a lookout platform in a yew tree. From this **vantage point,** we would watch for "The Enemy." Inside, on a stove made from an old lavatory cistern,[2] we would boil water for tea. The other place, my friend Mary and I named "Happy Hideout." It was a wildly overgrown depression between two fields which had once been a small **quarry**. We would spend whole days here in the summertime, setting off the rabbit traps placed by the local **gamekeeper** and cooking a lunch of stolen potatoes over a small campfire.

4   Perhaps The Hut represented a "masculine" need for boundaries, territory, and defensible space, whereas the other (where only girls played) fulfilled a more "feminine" need to nurture. We always cooked something and always sprung the iron traps with a big stick so no animals would be killed while we were there. The Hut has long since disappeared, vulnerable to the weather and natural decay. Happy Hideout is still there. On several nostalgic visits to that part of England, I have seen the cluster of trees that mark its location but have resisted the temptation to explore it more closely. I prefer to retain my memories and not discover—with adult perceptions—a perhaps rather ordinary place.

◆ After You Read

About the Content

1. Why do children have "secret places," according to the author?

2. In which cultures do children create secret places?

3. What were the differences between "The Hut" and "Happy Hideout"?

4. What does the author think these differences mean?

5. Why didn't the author want to revisit her childhood hideout?

About the Writing

1. Cooper Marcus uses lots of *description* in this short reading. Find places where you find effective descriptions.

2. How does the author use examples to illustrate her theories?

---

[2]**cistern**: a pot or container, usually made of metal.

U se pictures to help you visualize what you are going to write about. "A picture is worth a thousand words" is a familiar saying in English. Pictures, in fact, can help you when you are writing descriptions. Look at the picture of the house on page 44, which you discussed with your class. What words did you use to describe it? Would a picture of the "Happy Hideout" or "The Hut" in the previous reading have helped you understand Cooper Marcus's description even more?

Apply the Strategy

Think of your own "secret place." Draw a picture of it—include as much detail as you can remember. Don't worry about your drawing skills! Just try to get as much detail as you can into your drawing. Next, you will write a description of your drawing.

Create a Dominant Impression

Effective descriptions create an *impression,* or *feeling,* about the thing they describe. For example, if you wanted to describe a place that frightened you, you might use words that showed that feeling: *dark, spooky, eerie, threatening, dusty,* and so forth. Look at this description of a "secret place":

> There was an old shack on the hill behind Huber Park that was about to fall apart. About half the wallboards and most of the roof were missing. There was nothing to sit on but the rough board floor. It was totally surrounded by lush greenery, much of which extended inside through the missing wall planks. It really seemed to be out in the jungle. In reality, it was only about thirty feet or less from an asphalt path. A friend and I would sneak back there. We had to push the bushes and blackberry vines aside to gain entrance. Once inside, I remember it as being lush and cool—a very tranquil setting. My friend and I had a code word for it. We called it "The Palace."

Discuss these questions with your class:

- What impression does this description give you?

- What kind of place was "The Palace"?

One way that this writer makes the impression is by using *concrete* examples—that is, things you can see and feel through his writing. He doesn't just say they sat "on the floor," but on the "rough board floor." This gives the reader a clear mental *image* of the shack. Review the reading and find other examples of concrete images.

Can you make these phrases more concrete? Use your imagination. An example is given.

EXAMPLE: An ugly dress

REVISION: *An old green striped dress with coffee stains on the front, and two buttons missing*

> **Architecture is inhabited sculpture.**
>
> **—CONSTANTIN BRANCUSI**

1. A beautiful tree _____
   _____
   _____
   _____

2. A good book _____
   _____
   _____
   _____

3. A big building _____
   _____
   _____
   _____

4. A small dog _____
   _____
   _____
   _____

5. An interesting movie _____
   _____
   _____
   _____

Look at your drawing and think about the impression you want to give of your secret place. Then write a short description like the one on the previous page. Be sure to use concrete examples.

Next, you will apply your descriptive skills to a larger structure. Look at the photo on page 50. How would you describe this building? Discuss it with your classmates.

◆ Getting Ready to Read

TUNING IN: "Ice Hotel"

Watch the CNN video about the Ice Hotel. Discuss these questions with your class:

- Where is the hotel?
- How do guests get to the hotel?
- What are the guest rooms like?
- Would you enjoy staying at this hotel?

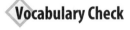

In your journal, respond to this question:

- Ice is an unusual material for a building. Think of another unusual building material, and describe a building that is made of it. Be creative! Share your writing with your classmates.

The next reading talks about the building in the photo on page 50, the Guggenheim Museum in Bilbao, Spain.

◆ Vocabulary Check

The words and phrases in this list are included in the reading. Check those that you know. Look up the ones you don't, or discuss them with a classmate. Then write a definition or an example sentence in your Vocabulary Log. The starred items are *professional vocabulary*, or words pertaining particularly to architecture, which will be discussed after the reading.

_____ atrium*   _____ chain-link fence*

_____ bungalow*   _____ constellation

_____ cavern   _____ corrugated metal*

_____ edifice*   _____ renovation

_____ exude   _____ repository

_____ iconoclast   _____ scaffolding*

_____ limestone   _____ titanium

_____ mammoth   _____ with a vengeance

_____ maverick

◆**Read**   **Reading 2: The "Miracle" of Bilbao**

1   BILBAO, Spain—This is the story of a marriage, one born less of love than convenience. Six years ago, the parties met. Bilbao, an industrial and often violent port city that is desperately seeking an image makeover, and the Solomon R. Guggenheim Foundation, a New York-based art superpower looking to expand its global presence.

2   However unlikely, the union has proved spectacularly fruitful. On October 19, 1997, the doors swung open at the Guggenheim Museum Bilbao, a sculpture of a building crafted in **titanium**, **limestone** and glass by controversial American architect Frank Gehry.

3   Architecture critics are tripping over themselves to invent new superlatives to praise the modern art **repository**; many settle on the word "miracle." Proud Bilbao officials are so confident of its international appeal that a new airport is in the works.

4   None of which surprises Tom Krens, the outspoken Guggenheim Foundation director who traveled to Bilbao twice a month for five years to oversee the birth of a star in what he calls the foundation's growing "**constellation**" of museums.

5   The **mammoth** 257,000 square-foot, $100-million **edifice** was financed by the Basque region, which has an independent government with its own budget. Bilbao is its major city. The museum will be both run by and showcase art for the Guggenheim Foundation. Only 1% of the foundation's collection of modern art is displayed at any one time because of space limitations.

6   The new museum will be home to some Spanish artists but mostly will feature modern masters including Mark Rothko and Andy Warhol.

7   But for the moment, the building is in the spotlight.

8   "That's by design. I wanted the museum to be architecturally and literally breathtaking. I wanted the greatest building of the 20th century," Krens says without bravado.[1]

9   Rising above the banks of Bilbao's murky Nervion River, the museum's twisting, restless form defies description. From one angle it squirms like fish in a basket; from another it

[1] **bravado**: boasting or bragging.

takes the form of a massive ocean liner. From across the Nervion, it is a rose with unfolding
10 silver petals.

Inside, the three-story building continues to bob and weave, with barely a straight line or right angle. The art, however, resides mostly in traditional, boxy white rooms. Size rules: The **atrium** soars to 165 feet; the "boat" gallery, which resembles the hold of a ship, is a vast
11 433-foot **cavern**.

Gehry's work here is as startling to the eye as the Eiffel Tower or Frank Lloyd Wright's 1959 screw-shaped Guggenheim. But while these two landmarks stand in contrast to their surroundings, the metallic tone of this new Guggenheim deliberately embraces the site's
12 past life as a shipyard.

Not far from its entrance, containers await loading. Across the street, rusted **scaffolding** clings to tired buildings. If visiting the original Guggenheim means strolling along posh Fifth Avenue, a trip here recalls New York's East River Drive, a mix of crumbling overpasses and
13 rough odors.

Here and throughout the city, Bilbao **exudes** both a sense of danger and excitement. Home to a million people, it is undergoing a $1.5 billion general **renovation**. It is also a long-term stronghold for ETA, a Basque separatist group that seeks independence from
14 Spain, sometimes through violent means.

So far, the museum has not been at risk. Officials don't expect that to change. They assume, and hope, that Basque pride is at work.
15

"This is a cultural project. It will be left alone," says Juan Ignacio Vidarte, director general of the Guggenheim Bilbao. "It has boosted our self-confidence and started a regeneration of the area. We want to project our real image
16 to the world."

Bilbao is trying **with a vengeance**. Its new subway system, designed by British architect Sir Norman Foster, is a gleaming, futuristic jewel that would make Paris or Washington, D.C., envious. A little upriver is a striking footbridge that looks more like a white sail than an overpass. A new music hall
17 also is in progress.

Today, the city has an infectious case of urban architecture. But one cannot overstate how odd the pairing of Bilbao and the Guggen-
18 heim was initially.

Bilbao became an unlikely home away from home for the **maverick** Gehry, infamous for enclosing his Santa Monica, California, **bungalow** in a disjointed frenzy of industrial materials such as **corrugated metal** and **chain-**
19 **link fence**.

In Spain, Krens provided Gehry with his ultimate commission, and Gehry would spare nothing to see that it represented a landmark
20 in a life's work.

Dozens of elaborate models were built at Gehry's Santa Monica offices. Engineering envelopes were pushed via a computer program called Catia, originally devised for the aerospace industry, which allows for mapping of
21 curved, three-dimensional surfaces.

The **iconoclast** even wound up watching the commodities markets;[2] when the price of titanium briefly dipped below that of alu-
22 minum, Gehry jumped.

The lighter and more durable metal was fashioned into the roof's scalelike panels: They absorb rather than reflect light and shudder in strong winds, both of which lend the building a
23 living, breathing quality.

The 68-year-old architect, whose other commissions include the forthcoming guitar-shaped Experience Music Project museum in
24 Seattle, seems pleased.

"If the building has iconic importance, and you can also hang paintings in it, I guess that's kind of an important place," Gehry says, adding, "It's really a miracle of collaboration between the Americans and the Basques."

---

[2] **commodities market**: the part of the financial market that reports the price of raw materials such as steel and titanium.

◆ After You Read

> The most beautiful things are those that madness prompts and reason writes.
>
> —ANDRE GIDE

About the Content

1. What has been the character of the city of Bilbao?

2. What material is the new museum made from?

3. How have the critics reacted to the building?

4. What kind of neighborhood is the new museum in?

5. What artists and types of art will be shown in the museum?

6. Who are the Basques?

7. What effect has the museum had on the city of Bilbao?

8. Who is Frank Gehry? What is he famous for?

About the Writing

1. Find descriptions of the museum itself. How do these descriptions use *concrete* images?

2. What kinds of *adjectives* does the author use to describe the museum? What impression do those adjectives give of the building?

3. Look at the photo of the Bilbao Guggenheim again (page 50). How does the description of the museum match the photo? Do you understand the description better by comparing it to the photo?

ACADEMIC POWER STRATEGY

Learn to use dictionaries effectively to help you in all areas of your studies. Dictionaries are an indispensable tool for writers, and learners of all kinds. Nearly everyone has used a dictionary, but there is more to learn to use a dictionary *well*. Dictionaries tell us not only what words mean, but sometimes how they are pronounced, how they look in context, where they originated, and what other forms they take.

Look at this dictionary entry from the *Newbury House Dictionary*:

1⟍   2⟍   3   4
glob·al /'gloubel/ *adj.* relating to all the world,
  worldwide: *We have a global economy today.* —— 5
6 —— *-adv.* **globally**; *-n.* **globalization**.

What information does this entry tell you?

1. Syllables: the entry is broken up into syllables, shown by the dot between **glob** and **al**.

2. Pronunciation: between the slashes (/) the word's pronunciation is shown. In addition, the stress on the word is shown by the apostrophe (').

3. Part of Speech: the abbreviation *adj.* tells you this form of the word is an *adjective*. Look at the beginning of the dictionary to learn the other abbreviations.

4. Definition: the definition of the word is given next.

5. Example: an example sentence is given to show how the word is used.

6. Related Forms: in this case, *globally,* is shown as an adverb form related to *global*.

This is a relatively simple entry. Many dictionary entries will contain multiple meanings for the same word. Some dictionaries, such as the *Oxford English Dictionary* and the *American Heritage Dictionary,* will give you a word's history as well.

Apply the Strategy

Look up a word that was new to you from the reading. Copy the dictionary definition as you find it in your dictionary. Explain each of the parts of the entry. Look up any other words from the reading that you don't understand.

LANGUAGE LEARNING STRATEGY

Learn the specialized vocabulary of a field or profession to write more accurately in that field. Each profession or field of study has specialized vocabulary. A doctor may speak of *hemoglobin*, a lawyer of *tort law*, a painter of *negative space*, and an architect of *atria* or *porticos*. When you are studying in a specialized area, you should learn its vocabulary so you can write about it with precision.

(continued on next page)

Apply the Strategy

Look at the starred items in the vocabulary list that came before the reading about Bilbao. These are words that are related to architecture. Look each of them up and write their definitions in your Vocabulary Log. When you write your own essay at the end of this chapter, try to use some of these words.

Try also to find a magazine pertaining to architecture, such as *Architectural Digest*. Read an article and look for new vocabulary that relates to architecture. Read the magazine's descriptions and think about how they describe different rooms of a house, or different parts of a building.

FROM READING TO WRITING

You have read two different descriptions: one of children's secret places, and one of the Bilbao Guggenheim. These descriptions focused on different kinds of buildings but sought to illustrate their ideas with words.

For your essay, you will also try to describe a building by using effective descriptive techniques.

◆Getting Ready to Write

In this essay, you will write a description of a building. Choose a building in your environment that interests you. It could be a campus building—a dormitory or library, for example. Or it might be an important building in your city.

You will do some research for this paper as well. After you choose your building, you will want to know some information about its history, appearance, and use.

How much of this information can you find out? You may not be able to get all the information, but try to find out as much as you can.

History

- When was it built?
- What is the name of the architect?
- What other buildings did he or she design?
- Is there anything unique about its history?

Appearance

- How big is it?
- What is it made of?
- Where is it located?
- What is its condition? (For example, is it new, well-kept, crumbling, etc.?)
- What color is it?
- What other things are important about its appearance?

Use

- What is the building used for?
- Does it have one use, or many?
- For this part, you might want to talk to one or two people who use the building. Ask them their thoughts on it. What is good about the building? What could be improved about the building? (If it's a building you use, you should think about these questions, too.)

◆Write

You're now ready to write your first draft. First, determine what *impression* you want to give of the building. Then choose an organizational plan. Remember to include *concrete* examples as you write your draft. The questions above can guide you in being specific in your examples.

After You Write

Revise

Refer to page 38 of Chapter 2 for help in revising your draft. Get feedback from a classmate on the strengths and weaknesses of your writing. Complete the table below, as you did in the previous chapter. Use your revision plan to guide your rewriting.

Feature	Problem	Possible Solution
Title		
Opening paragraph		
Description/ concrete examples		
Organization		
Word choice		
Conclusion		
Other		

Edit

After you have solved the problems identified in your revision plan, you can focus on editing and proofreading your paper. The editing phase includes double-checking your grammar, spelling, punctuation, and so forth. Remember, you can change this inventory as you progress.

Which of the following items do you think are a problem for you? Check the appropriate column.

PROBLEM	MAJOR PROBLEM	MINOR PROBLEM	NO PROBLEM	DON'T KNOW
Spelling	_____	_____	_____	_____
Punctuation	_____	_____	_____	_____

PROBLEM	MAJOR PROBLEM	MINOR PROBLEM	NO PROBLEM	DON'T KNOW
Subject–verb agreement	_____	_____	_____	_____
Verb tenses	_____	_____	_____	_____
Articles and prepositions	_____	_____	_____	_____
Plurals	_____	_____	_____	_____
Sentence fragments	_____	_____	_____	_____
Run-on sentences	_____	_____	_____	_____
Wordiness	_____	_____	_____	_____
Transitions	_____	_____	_____	_____
Relative clauses	_____	_____	_____	_____

If you have checked more than three as a "major problem," decide which three you would like to work on first. It's easier to concentrate on a few problem areas at a time.

The last step should be proofreading—that is, looking for misspellings, left-out words, and so forth as in the previous chapter. Before you turn your paper in, proofread it carefully.

Grammar You Can Use: Run-ons, Comma Splices, and Misused Conjunctions

A **run-on sentence** is a sentence that has two or more independent clauses that are not coordinated appropriately. You can either separate a run-on into separate sentences, or choose the appropriate coordinators or subordinators:

Run-on: I was reading a dull book it was a boring Saturday.

There are two sentences in this sentence that need to be made separate. Here are two options:

I was reading a dull book; it was a boring Saturday.
I was reading a dull book. It was a boring Saturday.

Joining two independent clauses with a comma is also usually incorrect. These types of sentences are called **comma splices**:

Comma Splice: I was reading a dull book, it was a boring Saturday.

These sentences are incorrectly joined with a comma. These sentences can be corrected in the same way the run-ons were. Or you might consider connecting them through subordination—showing more of a relationship between the two clauses:

I was reading a dull book, which made it a boring Saturday.

If you use coordination, you could join the sentences like this:

It was a boring Saturday and I was reading a dull book.

Incorrectly Joined Sentences

Correct the following sentences by inserting correct punctuation, reducing phrases, or making multiple sentences. If you find some to be already effective, leave them as they are. Be prepared to discuss your choices.

1. "I came, I saw, I conquered."—Julius Caesar

2. Unlike condominiums, houses require a lot of constant upkeep, they can take a lot of time.

3. I had never seen so many beautiful buildings in my life I was really impressed.

4. Construction of new museums has lagged in the latest economic downturn and libraries have also experienced this problem.

5. Many young people will become interested in the architectural field, they will work toward their degrees, and try to build better housing.

Self-Correction

In your recent essay, identify areas where you had difficulty with run-ons. Copy any sentences with run-on errors in them; then rewrite each sentence correctly. Review the section on fragments in Chapter 2, and correct any sentence fragments as well.

PUTTING IT ALL TOGETHER

The two plates on page 54, the Louvre Pyramid and the Pyramid of the Moon, both have similar architectural styles. Using the techniques you learned in this chapter, write a short description of these two structures. Be sure to use *concrete* descriptions and any architectural terminology you might have learned that fits into your description.

Write a dictionary-style definition for one of the terms you used in your description.

Test-Taking Tip

Ask questions about upcoming tests to better prepare yourself. Make a list of all the things you need to know about your test—how long is it, if you can use your notes or books, what material it covers, and so forth. Be sure you have the answers to all of your questions before the test date.

CHECK YOUR PROGRESS

On a scale of 1 to 5, rate how well you have mastered the goals set at the beginning of the chapter:

1 2 3 4 5   use pictures to help you visualize what you are going to write about.

1 2 3 4 5   understand the specialized vocabulary of a field or profession.

1 2 3 4 5   use dictionaries effectively.

1 2 3 4 5   avoid and fix run-ons, comma splices, and misused conjunctions.

1 2 3 4 5   (your own goal) _____

1 2 3 4 5   (your own goal) _____

If you've given yourself a 3 or lower on any of these goals:

- visit the *Tapestry* web site for additional practice.
- ask your instructor for extra help.
- review the sections of the chapter that you found difficult.
- work with a partner or study group to further your progress.

ook closely at the photos, and then discuss these questions with your classmates:

- What *processes* are the people in the photos involved in?
- Is there something you know how to do well?
- What would you like to learn how to do?

PROCESSES: SIMPLE MAGIC

Processes are everywhere. Whether simple processes, like making a cup of instant coffee, or more complicated ones, like performing a medical experiment, the things we do in our everyday lives are processes. Writing is a good way to explain a process. You tell your reader how something works or how something happened. When you write a procedure, you organize your writing in a very natural way; you follow an order that is already part of the activity.

Setting Goals

This chapter will provide you with some strategies and techniques for writing processes. You will learn how to:

◈ make outlines for both your reading and your writing.

◈ consider the audience for your writing.

◈ take notes effectively.

◈ organize your notes for a test.

◈ use *a*, *an*, and *the* accurately.

What other goals do you have for learning to write about processes? Write two more here.

_____

_____

Getting Started

Think about something that you know how to do well. It doesn't have to be complicated—maybe it's making a cake or fixing a flat tire on your bicycle. Try to explain that process to a classmate. When your classmate explains a process to you, ask questions about anything that isn't clear.

MEETING THE TOPIC

You can use a process to explain a scientific experiment, an historical event, or a practical activity. In this chapter, you will look at a "simple" process—how to eat using chopsticks, and a more complex natural one, how the moon came to be.

Good process writing tells *why* a process is important, not just *how* to do it.

Getting Ready to Read

The following reading explains the process of using chopsticks. Have you used chopsticks before? If so, how hard was it to learn to use them?

Vocabulary Check

The words and phrases in this list are included in the reading. Check those that you know. Look up the ones you don't, or discuss them with a classmate. Then write a definition or an example sentence in your Vocabulary Log.

_____ fabricate

_____ hamper (verb)

_____ industrial spy

_____ motor skill

_____ pivot (verb)

_____ splinter (verb)

_____ stationary

_____ stoop (verb)

_____ utensil

Read

Reading 1: Learn2[1] Use Chopsticks
Not the kind you play on the piano . . .[2]

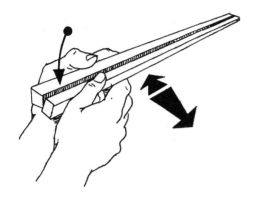

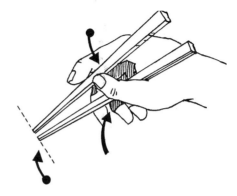

Before You Begin

What You'll Need

- Some small pieces of food
- A set of chopsticks—preferably tapered (has thick and thin end)

1   Would you eat a sandwich with a spoon? Or use a fork to eat ice cream? Certain foods taste better when eaten with the appropriate **utensil.** Chinese and Japanese foods are no exception: they taste better eaten with chopsticks. And although some of us were raised using chopsticks, it can be an awkward experience for the rest of us. Fortunately, learning to eat with chopsticks is a simple matter, as this 2torial shows.

2   Many of us labor under a misperception about chopsticks—that both sticks are moved together in your hand as you pick up a morsel. This is only half-true. Instead you'll be holding one chopstick in place while **pivoting** the other one to meet it. Simple, eh?

3   Heaven forbid that the restaurant serves disposable chopsticks in this era of disappear-

ing ancient forests. But to prepare you for that possibility, here's some advice on breaking them apart. Pull the sticks away from you on a horizontal plane, so your palms end up facing away from you. Twisting them apart vertically can cause **splintering,** which might **hamper** your dining experience.

Tips

4   • **Practice with a salad.** Start with large pieces and decrease the size as your skill improves. Soon you'll be plucking sesame seeds out of mid-air.
   • **Like any other** *motor skill,* **repetition is the key to success.** Several short sessions over a period of time is more effective than a big chunk of time.

Step 1. Position the Chopsticks

5   Place the first chopstick so that the thicker part rests at the base of your thumb and the thinner part rests on the lower side of your middle fingertip.

---

[1]Learn2 is the name of a web site (http://www.learn2.com) that teaches people how to do practical things. It is a play on the phrase *learn to*. The web site's lessons are called "2torials" instead of "tutorials."

[2]This refers to a simple piece of piano music called "Chopsticks."

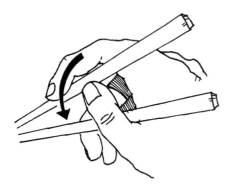

Next:

6 * Bring your thumb forward so that it traps the stick firmly in place. At least two or three inches of chopstick should extend beyond your fingertip.
  * Relax. Now position the other chopstick so that it is held against the side of your index finger by the end of your thumb.
  * Tap the ends of both sticks on the plate, while holding them at a slight angle to the table. Allow them to slide just a little so that the ends line up.

Step 2. Pivot the Top Chopstick

7 Place a little pressure on the top chopstick. It will pivot on your index finger just above the second knuckle. Remember: the bottom chopstick is **stationary**.

8 • The tip of the top chopstick will move towards the tip of the bottom chopstick. Encourage this. Hold those tips together firmly enough to grasp a piece of food and lift it off the plate. Place delicately into your waiting mouth. Although there's no need to **stoop,** you may wish to lean over your plate a bit during your first attempts. It might save you a clean-up.

9 That's about it. Have a little practice and you'll be able to **fabricate** stories about your life as an **industrial spy** in mainland China. Just remember to cook your rice so that it's sticky enough to pick up with the sides of the chopsticks. (For stickier rice, add a little extra water.)

◆ After You Read

About the Content

1. Why should people learn to use chopsticks?

2. What is the first step in learning to use chopsticks?

3. What is the second step?

4. How should you cook rice so that it can be eaten with chopsticks?

5. How should you hold the bottom chopstick?

6. Why should you practice motor skills?

About the Writing

1. This passage uses *humor* to convey its message. Locate sentences in the reading that are intended to be humorous, and underline them. Why do you think a writer would use humor in a process essay?

2. Does the writing tell why learning to eat with chopsticks is important?

3. How do the illustrations help you understand the process? Are illustrations important in this kind of writing?

4. Do you find this a clear and effective piece of writing? Why or why not?

5. A good measure of effective process writing is whether you can follow the instructions. If you can, get some chopsticks and practice, according to the directions. Were you able to follow the instructions?

> A journey of a thousand miles must begin with a single step.
>
> —CHINESE PROVERB

Quickwrite

Review the process you told your classmates about earlier in the chapter. Now write for 10 minutes about that process. (See page 5 for a review of the quickwrite process.) In writing, describe the process as completely as you can. Remember, don't worry yet about spelling, grammar, or punctuation.

ACADEMIC POWER STRATEGY

Take notes effectively to learn more efficiently and to remember more of your learning. Most instructors expect you to take notes on what you hear and what you do in class. Many people think that taking notes is a natural process that people know how to do "instinctively." Unfortunately, this isn't true. There are ways in which you can be a more efficient note taker:

- Identify the main ideas. Listen for phrases like "most importantly" or "in summary." These kinds of phrases give you clues that the information is worth making note of.

- Don't write everything you hear. Spending your time listening will help you to remember and understand better. If you are writing all the time, it will be difficult to pay attention to what the instructor is saying.

- Use a "recall column." Leave a blank column on your page to the left of your notes. After your class, go through your notes and summarize main ideas and important points in the blank column.

(continued on next page)

	Recall	Notes
	Main idea	Your notes go here. Write clearly and leave space.
	Listen	Remember to listen more than you write.

Apply the Strategy

In your next class, practice the note-taking tips listed in this strategy. Be sure to use a "recall column" in your notes to help you synthesize your ideas.

◇ Getting Ready to Read

In this reading, you will learn about a more complicated process: the formation of the earth's moon. As you read, pay attention to the *process* and to the ways in which the author uses description.

◇ Vocabulary Check

The words in this list are included in the reading. Check off the ones you know and look up the ones you don't, or discuss them with a classmate. Then write a definition or an example sentence in your Vocabulary Log.

_____ axis	_____ liquefy	_____ radioactive
_____ basalt	_____ molten	_____ slacken
_____ congeal	_____ momentum	_____ supposition
_____ granite	_____ oscillation	_____ tempestuous
_____ hinder		

Read

Reading 2: The Gray Beginnings

Rachel Carson

1   The events of which I write must have occurred somewhat more than two billion years ago. As nearly as science can tell, that is the approximate age of the earth, and the ocean must be very nearly as old. It is possible now to discover the age of the rocks that compose the crust of the earth by measuring the rate of decay of the **radioactive** materials they contain. The oldest rocks found anywhere on earth—in Manitoba[1]—are about 2.3 billion years old. Allowing 100 million years or so for the cooling of the earth's materials to form a rocky crust, we arrive at the **supposition** that the **tempestuous** and violent events connected with our planet's birth occurred nearly 2½ billion years ago. But this is only a minimum estimate, for rocks indicating an even greater age may be found at any time.

2   The new earth, freshly torn from its parent sun, was a ball of whirling gases, intensely hot, rushing through the black spaces of the universe on a path and at a speed controlled by immense forces. Gradually the ball of flaming gases cooled. The gases began to **liquefy,** and Earth became a **molten** mass. The materials of this mass eventually became sorted out in a definite pattern: the heaviest in the center, the less heavy surrounding them, and the least heavy forming the outer rim. This is the pattern which persists today—a central sphere of molten iron, very nearly as hot as it was 2 billion years ago, an intermediate sphere of semiplastic **basalt,** and a hard outer shell, relatively quite thin and composed of solid basalt and **granite.**

3   The outer shell of the young earth must have been a good many millions of years changing from the liquid to the solid state, and it is believed that, before this change was completed, an event of the greatest importance took place—the formation of the moon. The next time you stand on a beach at night, watching the moon's bright path across the water, and conscious of the moon-drawn tides, remember that the moon itself may have been born of a great tidal wave of earthly substance, torn off into space. And remember that if the moon was formed in this fashion, the event may have had much to do with shaping the ocean basins and the continents as we know them.

4   There were tides in the new earth, long before there was an ocean. In response to the pull of the sun the molten liquids of the earth's whole surface rose in tides that rolled **unhindered** around the globe and only gradually **slackened** and diminished as the earthly shell cooled, **congealed,** and hardened. Those who believe that the moon is a child of earth say that during an early stage of the earth's development something happened that caused this

[1]**Manitoba:** a province of central Canada.

rolling, viscid[2] tide to gather speed and **momentum** and to rise to unimaginable heights. Apparently the force that created these greatest tides the earth has ever known was the force of resonance, for at this time the period of the solar tides had come to approach, then equal, the period of the free **oscillation** of the liquid earth. And so every sun tide was given increased momentum by the push of the earth's oscillation, and each of the twice-daily tides was larger than the one before it. Physicists have calculated that, after 500 years of such monstrous, steadily increasing tides, those on the side toward the sun became too high for stability, and a great wave was torn away and hurled into space. But immediately, of course, the newly created satellite became subject to physical laws that sent it spinning in an orbit of its own about the earth.[3]

5   There are reasons for believing that this event took place after the earth's crust had become slightly hardened, instead of during its partly liquid state. There is to this day a great scar on the surface of the globe. This scar or depression holds the Pacific Ocean. According to some geophysicists, the floor of the Pacific is composed of basalt, the substance of the earth's middle layer, while all other oceans are floored with a thin layer of granite. We immediately wonder what became of the Pacific's granite covering and the most convenient assumption is that it was torn away when the moon was formed. There is supporting evidence. The mean[4] density of the moon is much less than that of the earth (3.3 compared with 5.5), suggesting that the moon took away none of the earth's heavy iron core, but that it is composed only of the granite and some of the basalt of the outer layers.

6   The birth of the moon probably helped shape other regions of the world ocean besides the Pacific. When part of the crust was torn away, strains must have been set up in the remaining granite envelope. Perhaps the granite mass cracked open on the side opposite the moon scar. Perhaps, as the earth spun on its **axis** and rushed on its orbit through space, the cracks widened and the masses of granite began to drift apart, moving over a tarry[5], slowly hardening layer of basalt. Gradually the outer portions of the basalt layer became solid and the wandering continents came to rest, frozen into place with oceans between them. In spite of theories to the contrary, the weight of geologic evidence seems to be that the locations of the major ocean basins and the major continental land masses are today much the same as they have been since a very early period of the earth's history.

[2]**viscid:** sticky, like glue.

[3]Carson is describing the moon.

[4]**mean:** average.

[5]**tarry:** like tar, thick and sticky.

 **After You Read**

About the Content

1. How old is the earth?

2. Which ocean does Carson think the moon came from?

3. What is her evidence?

4. Explain the process of the formation of the moon.

5. Where are the oldest rocks from?

6. How is the age of old rocks determined?

About the Writing

1. Carson uses small "processes-within-processes" in her writing. Locate one or two places where she uses this technique. How does it help your understanding?

2. How does Carson use *description* to enhance the explanation of the process?

3. Earlier in this chapter, you read that good process writing tells *why* a process is important. However, Carson does not do this. Does it matter? Why or why not?

TUNING IN: "The Iditarod Race"

Watch the CNN video about the Iditarod race. Discuss these questions with your class:

- What kind of race is the Iditarod and where does it take place?

- What is the tradition behind the race?

- What kind of *process* does the musher undertake to win the race?

- Would you enjoy participating in the Iditarod? Why or why not?

In your journal, respond to this question:

- Why do you think that people enjoy participating in "extreme sports"—sports that are very difficult and dangerous? Do you enjoy such sports?

FROM READING TO WRITING

You have read about different processes: a practical process—using chopsticks—and a scientific one—the formation of the earth's moon. For your paper, you will write about a process that you know well. You will also use a process to write your paper: outlining, drafting, and revising, before you submit your final draft.

◆ Getting Ready to Write

Make outlines for both your reading and your writing to understand the organization. An **outline** is a type of organization that gives you the key ideas. Outlining information you read can help you to understand the writer's organizational plan. Outlining your own writing plans will help you to become more organized. A formal outline looks like this:

I. Main idea after the Roman numeral *I*

   A. Idea of next importance, related to item *I*, put after a capital *A*

   B. Another idea supporting idea *I*, put after capital *B*

      1. An idea supporting item *B*, put after an Arabic numeral *1*

      2. A second idea supporting item *B*, put after an Arabic numeral *2*

II. Second main idea

and so forth.

When you are writing an outline to share with others, it is often a good idea to create a formal outline. However, when you are writing an outline as a plan for yourself, it is not necessary to use a formal outline. You might want just to list your ideas in order, or create some other kind of outline structure that works for you. For example, you might use this simple structure:

Plan for Writing

1. First idea here

2. Second idea next

3. Third idea

4. Closing

Apply the Strategy

Review the Carson reading passage. Fill in the missing information in the outline below. Each main point corresponds to a paragraph. Supply the details to support these points. The first one is done for you as an example.

I. The _____age_____ of the earth

    A. 2 billion years old

    B. Age of rocks

        1. Shown by radioactivity

        2. Oldest found in Manitoba

        3. Older ones might be found in the future

II. The _____ of the earth

III. The _____ of the moon

IV. The _____ of the tides

V. The _____ and the moon

VI. The influence of the _____ on the world

Write

> The process of writing has something infinite about it. Even though it is interrupted each night, it is one single notation.
>
> **—ELIAS CANETTI**

What process will you choose? You may want to elaborate on the one you have already talked and written about, or you might want to choose another topic. After you choose your topic, complete the following steps:

1. Write an outline that you will follow.

2. Include information on *why* this process is important.

3. Decide if illustrations or other supporting graphical material is helpful.

4. Write your first draft.

Before you start, you might want to look at this sample, written by a student. This paper tells the process of isolating fluorine, one of the earth's elements.

The Discovery of Fluorine

Fluorine is a yellowish, poisonous, highly corrosive halogen gas. However, it can be also be used for useful things like medicine, insecticides, and high-energy fuels. A scientist named Carl Scheele discovered it in 1771, but the isolation of fluorine challenged chemists for many years. It even took the lives of at least two scientists in the process.

The first attempt to free fluorine was done by a British chemist by the name of Humphry Davy, between the years 1811 and 1813. He first tried to liberate the element by using chemical methods, but failed. He then went on to try an electrolysis[1] process using batteries. The problem with this was that the electrolytes used either produced hydrogen and oxygen or fluoric acid in vapor form, making it difficult to study.

He then went on to make an electrochemical cell from horn silver because the hydrogen fluoride attacked glass. But this also failed—his hydrogen fluoride contained water. Even though Humphry discovered potassium, sodium, barium, strontium, calcium, and magnesium, his struggle to free fluorine was too much. Davy gave up.

---

[1]electrolysis: a chemical change brought about by using electric current.

Next two French scientists, Louis-Joseph Gay-Lussac and Louis-Jacques Thenard, created a liquid hydrogen fluoride free of water. But it didn't conduct the electricity needed for electrolysis. This ended their attempts to create fluorine.

In 1834, the famous physicist Faraday used the electrolysis of lead fluoride in platinum vessels to yield fluoride vapors. But after rigorous experimentation, he too failed. George Gore made a little fluorine through an electrolytic process but his apparatus exploded when the fluorine produced reacted with hydrogen from the other electrode.

Finally, a student of Faraday named Henri Moissan tried. He used electrolysis with hydrogen fluoride and Frémy's method. In 1886, the result was a yellow fluorine gas. His reward was the Nobel Prize for chemistry in 1906.

Several scientists' lives were lost in this search, not to mention the pain and suffering felt by chemists while strange chemicals ate through their vital organs. All of this was in the name of science, and the quest to find new elements.

LANGUAGE LEARNING STRATEGY

Consider the audience for your writing to help you to write more effectively. Who will read your writing? It may seem that in school, you are writing only for your teacher. However, as you've noticed, your classmates read your work, too. Perhaps you want to see your work published somewhere, or you want to write for another purpose. In all these cases you need to consider your audience. When you write a process, your audience is particularly important. If you want them to follow along with a procedure, they must be able to understand the steps. For example, if you want to tell them about an historical process, they must have the right background knowledge (or you must supply it in your writing).

(continued on next page)

Apply the Strategy   Review the readings in this chapter. Complete the table below.

READING	WHO IS THE AUDIENCE FOR THIS READING?	WHAT IS THE REQUIRED BACKGROUND KNOWLEDGE?
"Learn2 Use Chopsticks" (p. 63)		
"The Gray Beginnings" (p. 67)		
"The Discovery of Fluorine" (p. 72)		

After You Write

Revise

Give your draft to a classmate. Ask your reader for specific feedback on the process you describe. Ask your partner to *outline* your draft, and answer these questions:

1. Does the writing give the necessary background information (necessary materials, necessary information, etc.)?

2. Does it explain *why* the process is important, as well as what the process is?

3. Are any steps missing? Which ones?

4. Did any part of the process confuse you? Which one?

5. Where should there be more details supplied? Why?

Complete the following table, as you did in the previous chapter. Use your revision plan to guide your rewriting.

Feature	Problem	Possible Solution
Title		
Opening paragraph		
Logical ordering (clear plan)		
Word choice		
Conclusion		
Other		

(Also, refer to page 38 of Chapter 2 for help in revising your draft.)

Edit

After you have solved the problems identified in your revision plan, you can focus on editing and proofreading your paper. The editing phase includes double-checking your grammar, spelling, punctuation, and so forth. Remember, you can change this inventory as you progress.

Which of the items here and on the next page do you think are a problem for you? Check the appropriate column.

PROBLEM	MAJOR PROBLEM	MINOR PROBLEM	NO PROBLEM	DON'T KNOW
Spelling				
Punctuation				
Subject–verb agreement				
Verb tenses				
Articles				
Prepositions				

PROBLEM	MAJOR PROBLEM	MINOR PROBLEM	NO PROBLEM	DON'T KNOW
Plurals	_____	_____	_____	_____
Sentence fragments	_____	_____	_____	_____
Run-on sentences	_____	_____	_____	_____
Wordiness	_____	_____	_____	_____
Transitions	_____	_____	_____	_____
Relative clauses	_____	_____	_____	_____

If you have checked more than three as a "major problem," decide which three you would like to work on first. It's easier to concentrate on a few problem areas at a time.

The last step should be proofreading—that is, looking for careless mistakes: misspellings, leaving out words, typing words twice in a row, and so forth. Before you turn your paper in, proofread it carefully.

◈ Grammar You Can Use: Articles

Before nouns or noun phrases you can find the articles *a/an* or *the*, or no article at all. Determining which articles are appropriate is fairly simple for native speakers of English, but may be difficult if your native language is one that doesn't have an article system.

The following generalizations may help if you have problems with article use. However, there are exceptions to many, perhaps all, of these generalizations. Pay close attention to any unusual uses of articles you find in your reading and ask your instructor about them.

Generalization	Common Exceptions	Example
Single, countable nouns usually require an article.	When another type of determiner is used, such as a possessive, demonstrative, or quantifier.	a. There's *a car* in *the* driveway. b. That is her car.
Plural, specific, countable nouns usually require the article *the*.	If they refer to generic categories of items, do not use an article.	a. I put away the dishes. b. Dogs bark too much. (Note: this refers to all dogs, not a specific group.)
Abstract or generic nouns usually do not require an article.	When used as examples of specific instances, use an article.	a. Life is sweet. b. *The* life of *a* student is difficult.

> **If you can't describe what you are doing as a process, you don't know what you're doing.**
>
> **—W. EDWARDS DEMING**

Practice with Articles

Write the correct article (or *none*) in the blanks. Different articles may fit correctly. When you finish, discuss your answers with your classmates.

1. One of _____ smaller girls did _____ kind of puppet dance while her fellow clowns laughed at her. But _____ tall one, who was almost _____ woman, said something very quietly, which I couldn't hear.

   —Maya Angelou

2. I was born in _____ little village on _____ southeast coast. I was fifteen when we moved to _____ parcel of _____ land far away still on_____ same south coast. My mother was _____ widow.

   —Luz Alicia Herrera

3. By _____ time we had ridden _____ mile up-stream, _____ water was less than _____ foot deep and so crystal clear that we could see our herd of _____ several hundred carp still fleeing from _____ splashing, wading, horses.

   —Euell Gibbons

4. _____ processes to which _____ dead body may be subjected are after all to some extent circumscribed by _____ law. In _____ most states, for instance, _____ signature of _____ next of _____ kin must be obtained before _____ au-topsy may be performed, before _____ deceased may be cremated, before _____ body may be turned over to _____ medical school for _____ research pur-poses; or such _____ provision must be made in _____ decedent's will.

   —Jessica Mitford

5. For _____ Greeks, beauty was _____ virtue, _____ kind of excellence.

   —Susan Sontag

Self-Correction

In a recent piece of writing, identify areas where you had difficulty with articles. Copy any sentences with article errors in them, then rewrite each sentence correctly.

PUTTING IT ALL TOGETHER

◇**Use What You
Have Learned**

In this chapter, you have learned to make an outline, consider your audience, and take notes more effectively. In this activity, you will apply all of these new skills.

A "How-To" Demonstration

Give a short (5–10 minute) demonstration of something you know how to do, such as arrange flowers or fix a broken plate. Explain the process to your classmates as you demonstrate it. Here are the steps:

1. Write an outline for your presentation.

2. Assemble the materials you need.

3. Give your presentation, following your outline.

When other students give their presentations, take notes about the processes they describe.

Test-Taking Tip

Organize your notes to study more efficiently for tests. In order to get organized, the first thing you should do is make a list of all the things that will help you study, for example, your notes, some notecards, your textbook, your graded homework, and so forth. After you make your list, assemble all the things you'll use, and put them in one convenient location. Make special folders or labels to help you quickly identify the materials for your test. When you're ready to study, you'll have everything you need.

CHECK YOUR PROGRESS

On a scale of 1 to 5, rate how well you have mastered the goals set at the beginning of the chapter:

1 2 3 4 5   make outlines for both your reading and your writing.

1 2 3 4 5   consider the audience for your writing.

1 2 3 4 5   take notes effectively.

1 2 3 4 5   organize your notes for a test.

1 2 3 4 5   use *a*, *an*, and *the* accurately.

1 2 3 4 5   (your own goal) _____

1 2 3 4 5   (your own goal) _____

If you've given yourself a 3 or lower on any of these goals:

- visit the *Tapestry* web site for additional practice.

- ask your instructor for extra help.

- review the sections of the chapter that you found difficult.

- work with a partner or study group to further your progress.

L ook closely at the photo, and then discuss these questions with your classmates:

- What is happening in the photo?

- What are these people evaluating?

- Why is evaluation important in making purchases?

5

EVALUATION: COMPARING DIFFERENT VIEWS

Every day, you must make evaluations—they are central to thinking, speaking, and writing. As a student, you need to learn to evaluate books, films, historical events, artwork, your courses and teachers, and much more. People in the business world must evaluate products, ideas, job applicants, and more. In this chapter you will learn to evaluate ideas by using writing.

Setting Goals

This chapter will provide you with some strategies and techniques for using evaluation in your writing. You will learn how to:

◈ use comparisons and contrasts in your writing.

◈ find experts and sources in your community to help you locate information that you need for your studies.

◈ use quotations in your writing to help you communicate your ideas more strongly.

◈ write parallel structures effectively.

What other goals do you have for learning to use evaluation in your writing? Write two more here:

_____

_____

◆Getting Started

Are you interested in business? Discuss these questions with your classmates:

- What businesses are successful right now?
- What business interests you?

TUNING IN: "The Triple Trailer Truck"

© CNN

Watch the CNN video about the triple trailer truck. Discuss these questions with your class:

- What is a triple trailer truck?
- What opinion do many people have about this truck?
- What is the shipper's answer to these arguments?
- What is your opinion of this truck? Explain your answer.

In your journal, respond to this question:

- Would you enjoy truck driving as a career? Why or why not?

MEETING THE TOPIC

In this chapter, you will learn to make an evaluation and write about it effectively by using comparison techniques. In particular, you will examine topics of interest in business and learn to write about them analytically.

◆Getting Ready to Read

This reading looks at the practice of leasing equipment, rather than buying it, in business. As you read this passage, think about the reasons the author gives for leasing.

small truck

tractor truck

sports utility vehicle (SUV)

Vocabulary Check

The words and phrases in this list are included in the reading. Check the ones you know. Look up the ones you don't, or discuss them with a classmate. Then write a definition or an example sentence in your Vocabulary Log.

_____ capital	_____ depreciate	_____ logistics
_____ cash flow	_____ fleet (noun)	_____ offset
_____ CEO	_____ liability	_____ tax write-off
_____ climes	_____ lessee	_____ turning radius
_____ daily rounds		

Read

Reading 1: Leasing Passes the Road Test, Part I

by Julie Candler

1   A new **fleet** of heavy-duty trucks arrived at PWS Foods, Inc., in Grand Prairie, Texas, in 1993. Since then, the refrigerated trucks have made daily deliveries to supermarkets, convenience stores, restaurants, and food services, supplying customers in the warm **climes** of northern Texas with cold treats such as national brands of ice cream and other frozen desserts.

2   PWS had been leasing trucks from three companies but decided in 1993 to simplify **logistics** by using just one. After the dessert distributor switched to PACCAR Leasing (known as PacLease) of Bellevue, Washington, it discovered another advantage to its new arrangement.

3   "We liked the fact that we were able to get a whole new fleet," says Arnold O. Felner, executive vice president for administration at PWS, which generally has about 75 employees. "There's no way that a company our size could invest in vehicles and have enough **capital** to run a business."

4   Another benefit of leasing cars and light- and heavy-duty trucks is relief from the responsibility of servicing the vehicles.

5   PWS, like many other companies with fleets of heavy-duty trucks, contracts for full-service leasing. "We like the convenience of having repair and maintenance service available 24 hours a day, seven days a week" for the company's 30 Mack, UD, and Peterbilt trucks, says Felner.

6   PacLease mechanics visit the firm nightly to do routine maintenance, wash the vehicles, and check the refrigeration units. "It's important because ice cream can go bad in 20 minutes," Felner says.

7   Full service frees the **lessee** from environmental and regulatory concerns as well. When a firm such as PWS operates its own shop for fueling and servicing vehicles, it takes on the burden of conforming with regulations such as those on disposal of toxins. With full-service leasing, PacLease assumes the risk for any **liability** or violation connected with these regulations.

8   Felner also likes the flexibility that leasing offers in scheduling routes and loads. "When we have an occasional need for a tractor–trailer combination for a special job," he says, "PacLease provides it."

9   PacLease helped determine the specifications of components such as transmissions for PWS's new trucks, says Felner. "We told them our needs—like trucks with a short **turning radius** to pull up to the backs of stores—and they came up with the right vehicles."

10   Another company that has benefited from full-service leasing is DiCarlo Food Services, Inc., in Holtsville, New York. DiCarlo dropped vehicle ownership and in-house maintenance last July and contracted with Miami-based Ryder System, Inc., for full-service leasing.

DiCarlo's 33 trailer-hauling tractors and five medium-duty trucks distribute meat, produce, and frozen foods to restaurants and food services in the New York City area.

11 Ryder routes two maintenance people each day to DiCarlo. "One mechanic arrives at 4 P.M. to work on vehicles returning from their **daily rounds**," says Anthony Yodice, DiCarlo's vice president of operations. "Another shows up at 4 A.M. to be certain each loaded truck starts and is ready to make early-morning deliveries as scheduled."

12 Scott Saperstein, marketing coordinator at DiCarlo, says that "initial figures show leasing is far superior to what we had before. It's more cost-effective, and we get greater productivity from the drivers."

Increased Efficiency

13 As president and **CEO** of the Truck Renting and Leasing Association in Alexandria, Va., J. Michael Payne can cite other advantages for businesses that lease their trucks. Truck-leasing companies, he says, are putting the most fuel-efficient, safest, lowest-maintenance, and most environmentally friendly trucks available onto the nation's highways.

14 "Their customers are operating fleets that aren't any more than four to five years old," Payne says. "Some fleets are getting smaller because they get more-efficient information and management systems through lease companies. That enables them to get more work done with fewer vehicles.

15 "In addition, lease-company experts provide technology and other expertise so their customers' personnel can devote resources to being in retailing or whatever their business is," says Payne. "Leasing companies today offer servicing, registration, handling of taxes, and fuel-system management."

16 Even though the leased vehicles are not on the lessee company's books, the monthly leasing fees can be debited as a business expense. Explains Rodney J. Couts, executive director of the independent lessors who make up the National Vehicle Leasing Association (NVLA) in Burlingame, California: "For most businesses, leasing equates to a higher **tax write-off**. They can write off the cost of payments, which usually exceeds what the cost of depreciation would be for vehicles if a company owned them."

17 Raymond L. Smith, president of U.S. Fleet Leasing in San Mateo, California, says leasing is "a better use of **cash flow** versus putting out the full purchase price. Lessees can use that money to invest in their business without investing valuable capital, an asset that's **depreciating** and is not going to make any money for them."

18 PWS and DiCarlo Food reflect a national trend toward increased leasing of commercial cars and trucks. "The largest increase is in the fleets of less than 100 units," says Smith. "Small-business fleets are growing faster." U.S. Fleet Leasing specializes in serving small and midsize companies with fleets of 10 to 200 cars or trucks.

19 One of the biggest changes in leasing, says David P. LaFever, executive director of the National Automotive Fleet Association (NAFA) in Iselin, New Jersey, is an increased interest among large leasing companies in supplying fleets of 25 to 50 vehicles. "Some may even go a little bit smaller," he adds.

20 The growth in leasing is largely attributable to affordability, says the NVLA's Couts. "As prices get higher and higher [for new cars and trucks], leasing can **offset** the increases."

21 Leasing as a share of production was 24 percent in 1993, and the percentage has risen steadily since. A late-1996 NAFA survey of managers of commercial and publicly owned fleets found that they leased 34 percent of their vehicles.

22 Last year, the Truck Renting and Leasing Association's 757 member companies registered more than 44 percent of all the new heavy-duty trucks in classes 6, 7, and 8 (gross vehicle weights of more than 19,500 pounds) that were placed in commercial service in the United States, says Payne.

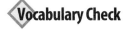 **After You Read**

About the Content

1. What advantages are there in leasing trucks, according to the article?

2. Why is full-service leasing advantageous?

3. Why is truck leasing "environmentally friendly"?

4. How does leasing affect taxes?

5. What is one of the biggest changes in leasing, according to David LaFever?

6. How much has leasing grown recently? Why has leasing grown, according to the article?

About the Writing

1. For whom do you think this article was written?

2. How is this article organized? Whom does the article quote? Do you think this is effective?

3. How do quotations help you understand the article?

Getting Ready to Read

Now you will read the second part of the article, which presents some of the disadvantages of leasing. As you read, think about these disadvantages in comparison to what you have just read.

Vocabulary Check

The words in this list are included in the reading. Check those that you know. Look up the ones you don't, or discuss them with a classmate. Then write a definition or an example sentence in your Vocabulary Log.

_____ acquisition   _____ open-end

_____ fluctuation   _____ presuppose

_____ logistics   _____ stipulate

_____ modular   _____ testimonials

 Read

Reading 2: Leasing Passes the Road Test, Part II

Two Types of Endings
....

1 To offset the rising cost of vehicles, H. Roger Knape focuses on maintaining as high a resale price as possible on cars leased for Knape & Vogt Manufacturing Co., a furniture-hardware producer in Grand Rapids, Michigan. Knape & Vogt uses **open-end** leasing, an arrangement in which the lessee is responsible for the market value of the vehicle when it is sold at the end of

the lease. Open-end deals are the most popular among firms that lease fleets because they ultimately have the lowest cost.

2   "I learned through experience that the cost of fleet operation is as much a factor of resale price as it is of **acquisition** at the other end," says Knape, the company's administrative coordinator for sales. He emphasizes vehicle care for obtaining a good end-of-lease price.

3   Knape & Vogt sales and management personnel nationwide use the 28 cars and three minivans the company leases from Emkay, Inc., of Itasca, Illinois, and Nationsbanc Leasing Corp. of Tucker, Georgia.

4   Knape and other fleet managers capitalize on **fluctuations** in used-car prices to maximize return on vehicles. Knape avoids trading in autos during December or the early months of a year, when resale values are traditionally low.

5   An alternative to open-end leasing that is more attractive to some small firms is a closed-end lease, in which the lessor is responsible for depreciation. The lessor charges the customer based on estimates for depreciation, maintenance, insurance, and registration, plus a management fee. The market value of the vehicle at the end of the lease term belongs to the lessor. The customer is liable only for lease payments.

6   Closed-end leases are considered the easiest for budgeting and controlling costs. However, they carry a penalty if the mileage **stipulated** in their 24- or 36-month terms is exceeded.

7   Closed-end leasing works well for G.S. Blodgett Corp. of Burlington, Vermont, because the company's vehicles seldom exceed the 50,000-mile limit under the three-year leases. Blodgett leases 40 vehicles from U.S. Fleet Leasing, mostly for use by sales and executive personnel.

8   Two pickups and a van haul materials among factories in Burlington, where Blodgett manufactures commercial convection, conveyor, and other ovens for customers such as Pizza Hut.

9   Emilie Mattesich, fleet manager and executive assistant to the president of Blodgett, says she prefers closed-end leasing because pay-

ments are easy to budget. "We typically pay $375 monthly for the term of the lease. We possibly could get a better price for the vehicle on resale with an open-end lease, but we don't want to get into the resale business."

An Ownership Advocate

10   Despite the numerous **testimonials** to the advantages of leasing, ownership and in-house repairs of a fleet can pay off, according to the calculations of Ken Higgins of J.F. Fick, Inc., an Anheuser-Busch beer distributor in Fredericksburg, Virginia.

11   Higgins, the company's director of transportation, employs mechanics who keep the firm's 35 Navistar tractors running dependably for an average of 12 years, at about 15,000 miles per year. Some of J.F. Fick's 31 light trucks, mostly Ford Aerostar minivans and Ford Explorer sport-utility vehicles used by supervisors, have accumulated 300,000 miles. "We have few breakdowns," says Higgins.

Light Trucks on the Rise

12   Many fleets that had been composed mainly of cars are now leaning toward trucks as the popularity of pickups, minivans, and sport-utility vehicles increases.

13   Strong resale value is one reason the number of light trucks increased by 15.8 percent in 1996 among the nation's top 100 commercial fleets, according to the trade publication *Automotive Fleet.* At Follett Corp., a River Grove, Illinois, company that owns college bookstores and distributes textbooks, midsize cars make up 60 percent of the company's 220-vehicle fleet; minivans account for the remainder, and their share is increasing each year. Ruth Alison, who handles the firm's fleet, leases all the vehicles from Automotive Rentals Inc., in Mount Laurel, New Jersey, under a plan that includes regular and emergency maintenance and the handling of taxes. And although she pays $200 to $300 more ini-

tially for minivans with a third seat, "it's not a problem," she says, because the seat raises resale values by $500 to $800.

Heavy-Duty Packages
....

14 In the heavy-duty-truck area, the trend among leasing companies is toward tailoring a package for each customer. "The days when you would take a lease package off the shelf and write a program with the customer are over," says Payne of the Truck Renting and Leasing Association.

15 "Now it's **modular** capabilities," says John Haddock, vice president of marketing for Ryder Transportation Services, a division of Ryder System. "We might finance-lease part of a fleet, then provide some full-service leasing and some dedicated-contract carriage."

16 Under dedicated-contract carriage, a firm contracts to supply trucks, drivers, other labor, management, and computer-based systems for routing and tracking. The arrangements are often coupled with "**logistics** design" for routing and distribution. Use of dedicated-contract carriage is increasing, according to firms that provide the service, and most truck-leasing companies are offering it or are partnering with other companies that do.

17 "It's no longer just moving goods from point A to point B," says Haddock. "Companies are winning by the quality of their supply chain as well as the quality of their product. . . . We don't **presuppose** a solution. We want to figure out what a customer needs and satisfy those needs by adding [choices] among those modules. We are trying to broaden our range because we recognize that customers don't come in one standard size."

After You Read

About the Content

1. What is open-ended leasing? Why is this type of plan popular?
2. How can businesses receive a good "end-of-lease price"?
3. Why doesn't Roger Knape trade in his cars in December or January?
4. What is a closed-end lease? What are the advantages and disadvantages?
5. What are the advantages of owning your own fleet, according to the article?
6. Why are light trucks becoming popular?
7. What does John Haddock mean by "modular capabilities"?
8. What does "dedicated-contract carriage" mean?

About the Writing

> **Comparisons are odious.**
>
> —JOHN DONNE

1. How does the article introduce the disadvantages of leasing?
2. Compared to the advantages, what proportion of the article is devoted to disadvantages? What can you conclude from this?
3. How would you describe the style of this article? Why do you think the author chose this style?

FROM READING TO WRITING

You have read about evaluation within the trucking industry, and how business owners evaluate their own needs for services. For your paper, you will also evaluate a product in order to recommend its purchase. You will use techniques of comparing and contrasting to write your essay.

LANGUAGE LEARNING STRATEGY

Use comparisons and contrasts to help you evaluate ideas in writing. Comparisons show similarities among things or ideas; contrasts show differences. Typically, when evaluating ideas or products, you will need to make both comparisons and contrasts. A good comparison/contrast shows not only the points of comparison, but also the purpose for doing so.

Apply the Strategy

Review the readings and your responses to the discussion questions. Complete the chart below to compare leasing delivery vehicles to buying them. Add any ideas you think of that aren't included in the reading.

Benefits of Leasing	Benefits of Buying

◇Getting Ready to Write

Imagine that you need to recommend a product or service to a company you work for. It can be any product that interests you. Here are some suggestions. Brainstorm to come up with ideas to add to the list:

- computers: laptop or desktop?
- copy machines: low cost or high speed?
- child care: in-home babysitter or day-care center?
- medical insurance: health maintenance organization or individual plan?

- _____
- _____
- _____

Begin to gather information about the product or service you chose.

ACADEMIC POWER STRATEGY

Find experts and sources in your community to help you locate information you need to succeed in your studies. Everyone has an area of expertise. From the president of a bank to a child-care worker, each person knows how to do his or her job. Many of your classes will require you to talk to or locate people who have areas of expertise different from your own. Knowing how to contact these people—through the telephone, by letters, or by e-mail—can make your studies easier.

Apply the Strategy

Look at the topic you chose for your paper. Make a list of five sources you can use to support your ideas and get information. Work with a partner if you need help listing ideas. Write them in this table.

Information I Need	What Experts or Sources Might Provide This Information

◆**Write**

> There are as many ways to look upon a thing as there are men to look upon it. That, my son, is what the truth is.
>
> —*NATIVE AMERICAN SHAMAN IN INDIAN AMERICA* **BY JAMAKE HIGHWATER**

Organizing Comparison/Contrast Essays

There are two basic organizational strategies for a comparison/contrast essay. These are the "whole-to-whole" method and the "point-by-point" method. Consider a situation in which you would compare apples and oranges.

Whole-to-Whole

In the whole-to-whole method, after stating the main purpose of writing, the writer explains all the features of apples first, then all the features of oranges. The conclusion summarizes the important issues. Look at this outline:

I. Introduction

II. Features of Apples

    A. Color: Green, red, yellow
    B. Shape: Somewhat round
    C. Size: Small to large

III. Features of Oranges

    A. Color: Orange
    B. Shape: Round
    C. Size: Fairly uniform

IV. Conclusion

Point-by-Point

In point-by-point organization, both apples and oranges are evaluated in each paragraph. The topics of the paragraphs become the features themselves.

I. Introduction

II. Color

    A. Apples: Green, red, yellow
    B. Oranges: Orange

III. Shape

    A. Apples: Somewhat round
    B. Oranges: Round

IV. Size

    A. Apples: Small to large
    B. Oranges: Fairly uniform

V. Conclusion

Point-by-point comparison or contrast is more common than whole-to-whole, as it makes it easier for a reader to concentrate on the similarities and differences. However, both organizational methods work well.

- Which method was used in the readings in this chapter?

- Do you think this was an effective organizational plan? Why or why not?

- What method will you use in your paper?

- Create a chart like that found on page 88 to organize your comparisons and contrasts before writing.

LANGUAGE LEARNING STRATEGY

Use quotations in your writing to help you to communicate your ideas more strongly. As a writer, you aren't expected to be an expert in everything you write about, but you do need to consult experts. You noticed in the reading that the writer used quotations, or the words of others, to support the ideas the writer was presenting. This practice shows that the writer has done the appropriate research and has read or talked to people who are experts or have experience in the subject. In "Leasing Passes the Road Test," the writer talked to a number of businesspeople about their practices in leasing and included *quotations* from these people.

Apply the Strategy

Look at the quotations in these paragraphs from "Leasing Passes the Road Test, Parts I & II."

1. "We liked the fact that we were able to get a whole new fleet," says Arnold O. Felner, executive vice president for administration at PWS, which generally has about 75 employees. "There's no way that a company our size could invest in vehicles and have enough capital to run a business."

(continued on next page)

2. Ryder routes two maintenance people each day to DiCarlo. "One mechanic arrives at 4 P.M. to work on vehicles returning from their daily rounds," says Anthony Yodice, DiCarlo's vice president of operations. "Another shows up at 4 A.M. to be certain each loaded truck starts and is ready to make early-morning deliveries as scheduled."

3. Scott Saperstein, marketing coordinator at DiCarlo, says that "initial figures show leasing is far superior to what we had before. It's more cost-effective, and we get greater productivity from the drivers."

What do you notice about the quotations? Discuss these questions:

- What verb tense is used for the verb *say*? Why?
- How are the speakers identified? Why?

Grammar You Can Use: Parallel Structures

Writing comparisons and contrasts often calls for writing sentences with parallel structures. Look at these sentences:

- A job in sales is easier to get than a job in engineering.
- Restaurants are more plentiful in the city than in the suburbs.
- In my new job, I have to stock shelves, check prices, and help the manager.

> Choice has always been a privilege of those who could afford to pay for it.
>
> —ELLEN FRANKFORT

The underlined words in each of the sentences are parallel; that is, they are of the same form. Errors in parallel structure can lead to confusion for your readers. Look at these examples, in which there are errors in parallel structure. How are these sentences confusing? Rewrite them correctly.

1. The buildings in New York are higher than San Francisco.

   _____

2. The parking problem in San Francisco is more severe than Los Angeles.

   _____

   _____

3. The assistant manager is responsible for keeping personnel records, unlocking the store, overseeing marketing, and must work eight hours a day.

_____

_____

◆ After You Write

Revise

Give your draft to a classmate. Ask your reader for specific feedback on your comparison. Ask your partner to answer these questions:

1. Does the writing give the reason for the comparison/contrast?
2. Is it clear which organizational plan the writer used?
3. Do the comparisons make sense?
4. Are parallel structures used correctly?
5. Does the writer use quotations to illustrate and support the main ideas?

Now complete the table below, as you did in the previous chapter. Use your revision plan to guide your rewriting.

Feature	Problem	Possible Solution
Title		
Opening paragraph		
Logical ordering (clear plan)		
Correct use of parallel structures		
Word choice		
Conclusion		
Other		

(Also, refer to page 38 of Chapter 2 for help in revising your draft.)

Edit

After you have solved the problems identified in your revision plan, you can focus on editing and proofreading your paper. The editing phase includes double-checking your grammar, spelling, punctuation, and so forth. Each student has unique problems in this area, so it may be helpful to take an inventory of problem spots, based on your past experience as a writer. Remember, you can change this inventory as you progress.

Which of the following items do you think are a problem for you? Check the appropriate column.

PROBLEM	MAJOR PROBLEM	MINOR PROBLEM	NO PROBLEM	DON'T KNOW
Spelling	_____	_____	_____	_____
Punctuation	_____	_____	_____	_____
Subject–verb agreement	_____	_____	_____	_____
Verb tenses	_____	_____	_____	_____
Articles	_____	_____	_____	_____
Prepositions	_____	_____	_____	_____
Plurals	_____	_____	_____	_____
Sentence fragments	_____	_____	_____	_____
Run-on sentences	_____	_____	_____	_____
Wordiness	_____	_____	_____	_____
Parallel structures	_____	_____	_____	_____

If you have checked more than three as a "major problem," decide which three you would like to work on first. It's easier to concentrate on a few problem areas at a time.

The last step should be proofreading—that is, looking for careless mistakes: misspellings, leaving out words, typing words twice in a row, and so forth. Before you turn your paper in, proofread it carefully.

PUTTING IT ALL TOGETHER

In this chapter, you have learned to find information from experts, quote sources, make comparisons, and write parallel sentences. Think about these skills as you do the following activity.

Would you like to make a major purchase, such as a car or computer? Find an advertisement for a major item you would like to buy. Bring in the advertisement and present it to your class. Discuss the pros and cons of making the purchase.

Test-Taking Tip

Use flash cards to study for tests. Flash cards are useful study tools because they are easy to make and easy to carry. When you have a test, write important facts, ideas, and questions on flash cards. When you have a few free minutes between classes or after lunch, test yourself on the information on your flash cards. Use them with a study group to test each other as well.

CHECK YOUR PROGRESS

On a scale of 1 to 5, rate how well you have mastered the goals set at the beginning of the chapter:

1 2 3 4 5   use comparisons and contrasts in your writing.

1 2 3 4 5   find experts and sources in your community to help you locate information you need for your studies.

1 2 3 4 5   use quotations in your writing to help you communicate your ideas more strongly.

1 2 3 4 5   write parallel structures effectively.

1 2 3 4 5   (your own goal) _____

1 2 3 4 5   (your own goal) _____

If you've given yourself a 3 or lower on any of these goals:

- visit the *Tapestry* web site for additional practice.

- ask your instructor for extra help.

- review the sections of the chapter that you found difficult.

- work with a partner or study group to further your progress.

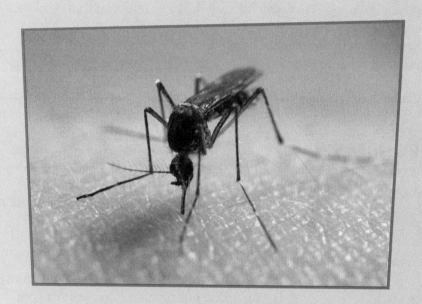

L ook closely at the photo, and then discuss these questions with your classmates:

- Do you know what malaria is?
- Where could you find information about malaria?
- Why is informative writing important in the medical field?

6

INFORMING: DISEASES THAT AFFECT US

Informative writing gives readers information that they will find helpful. There are many kinds of informative writing: journalism, research papers, and instruction manuals, for example, all give information. However, all types of informative writing share one feature—they organize facts and data in a format that will be understood clearly. In this chapter, you will work with writing in the fields of science and medicine, focusing on how information is organized and presented so that readers can make sense of technical material.

Setting Goals

This chapter will provide you with some strategies and techniques used in informative writing. In this chapter you will learn how to:

◈ think about your purpose for writing in order to write in a more focused way.

◈ familiarize yourself with what is in your library to do research more efficiently.

◈ use library resources to make your essays stronger and more informative.

◈ use prepositions correctly.

What other goals do you have for learning about analytical writing? Write two more here:

_____

_____

◆Getting Started

Before you begin the chapter, take a few minutes to write down what you know about informative writing. You can begin by answering these questions:

1. What kind of informative writing do you read? Why?

2. Do you read the newspaper regularly? Why or why not?

3. What do you already know about informative writing?

LANGUAGE LEARNING STRATEGY

Apply the Strategy

Think about the purposes for writing to write in a more focused way. Writers have reasons for writing their stories. Understanding what the reasons for writing are can make you a better writer because you will have a clear goal in mind as you write.

Look at the following purposes for writing. Then match the type of writing with its purposes by writing the letters in the blanks. Next, provide a brief explanation. A type of writing can have more than one purpose. The first one is done as an example.

Some purposes for writing:

A. to inform

B. to entertain

C. to persuade

D. to explain a process

E. to argue

Some Types of Writing	Explanation
<u>A</u> <u>B</u> <u>D</u> a recipe	A recipe informs us about a dish, it explains the process of how to prepare a dish from beginning to end, and it can also be entertaining, especially if it tells us something about the history of the dish.
___ ___ ___ a math textbook	

Some Types of Writing	Explanation
__ __ __ a magazine advertisement for a car	
__ __ __ a letter to a family member	
__ __ __ a short story	
__ __ __ a magazine article about online banking	
__ __ __ a political pamphlet	

Getting Ready to Read

The first reading describes how malaria is transmitted. It contains a lot of scientific language about the disease, but with the use of diagrams and definitions within the text, it clearly shows how this disease affects us.

Vocabulary Check

The words and phrases in this list are included in the reading. Check the ones you know. Look up the ones you don't, or discuss them with a classmate. Then write a definition or example sentence in your Vocabulary Log.

_____ amoeba	_____ engulf	_____ parasite
_____ chemotherapy	_____ gland	_____ periodicity
_____ circulatory system	_____ hemoglobin	_____ proliferate
_____ coalesce	_____ matrix	_____ replicate
_____ cyst	_____ myriad	_____ rigor
_____ discrete	_____ nucleus	_____ synchrony

Many of these words, particularly the scientific terms, will be defined within the reading.

Read

Reading 1: The Malaria Capers

by Robert S. Desowitz

Malaria: From the Miasma to the Mosquito

1 The infection in humans begins when an infected female anopheline mosquito (only the lady mosquito partakes of blood; the male, gentle fellow that he is, flies about in a lifelong pursuit of sex and nectar) injects into the bloodstream, during the act of feeding, threadlike malaria **parasites** (the *sporozoites*) that have been stored in her salivary **glands.** Thousands of sporozoites are usually injected (Figure 1) and they are carried in the bloodstream to the liver, where they leave the **circulatory system** and each sporozoite penetrates a "building block" cell of the liver tissue. Within the liver cell the sporozoite rounds up and transforms into a "spore." For about two weeks this spore **replicates** repeatedly (a process known as *schizogony*), until there are many thousand "spores" (*merozoites*) within a **cystlike** structure, the host liver cell having been destroyed by the **proliferating** parasites (Figure 2).

2 Those two weeks are a clinically quiescent[1] period for the person within whom the seeds of malaria are undergoing repeated division. There is no fever, no sign of the illness that is to descend so swiftly. The first clinical attack—the intense **rigor** and sweating with high fever—develops when the cyst bursts to the **myriad** of "spores" (merozoites) into the bloodstream (Figure 3). Each merozoite now attaches to the surface of a red blood cell and then enters it. Inside the red blood cell the young parasite appears as a minute circlet with a **nucleus**-dot (the ring stage). The parasite feeds avidly by **engulfing,** in **amoeba**-like fashion, the red cell's **hemoglobin.** The parasite grows the "body" cytoplasm, increasing until it fills more than half the red cell (the *trophozoite* stage).

3 The next developmental event is the asexual "shattering" of the nucleus (*schizogony*) into eight to twenty-four **discrete** bits (the number depending on the species of malaria parasite) within the cytoplasmic **matrix.** There then occurs a complex reorganization in which the cytoplasm **coalesces** around each nuclear bit to form a "spore," that is, a merozoite. The demolished red cell bursts; the merozoites are released into the bloodstream to attack and invade new red blood cells.

[1]**quiescent:** quiet.

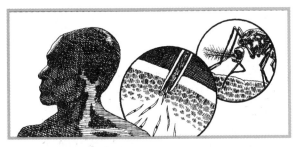

Figure 1

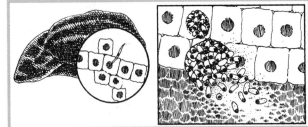

Figure 2

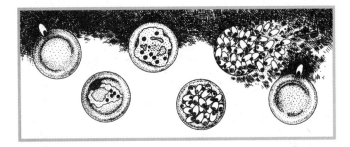

Figure 3

4   This process is repeated over and over again with more and
more red cells becoming parasitized until natural or acquired im-
munity, or antimalarial **chemotherapy,** or death (in the case of
untreated *Plasmodium falciparum* infections in non-immunes)
brings the repetitive process to an end. Moreover, there is a marvelous **synchrony** in development. The growing malaria parasites
are a *corps de ballet*[2] moving together in their growth cycle; all are
at the ring stage simultaneously, all are at the trophozoite[3] stage
simultaneously, all burst, as merozoites[4], from their millions of in-
vaded red blood cells simultaneously. This synchronicity of development is responsible for the characteristic **periodicity** of malarial
fever cycles in the infected human; the forty-eight hours between
fever peaks for *Plasmodium falciparum, Plasmodium vivax,* and
Plasmodium ovale, and seventy-two hours between peaks for
Plasmodium malariae malaria.

◆**After You Read**

About the Content

1. How long does it take for the symptoms of malaria to show?
   Why?

2. Which type of mosquito is responsible for malaria?

[2]***corps de ballet:*** group of ballet dancers.
[3]**trophozoite:** a parasite in a resting state.
[4]**merozoite:** a parasite that is ready to reproduce.

3. Summarize the process by which malaria is transmitted. Use chronological order (see Chapter 4 to review writing about processes).

About the Writing

1. Desowitz uses some vocabulary that might be difficult for the average reader. Why does he do so? How does he make the reading easier?

2. Who is the audience for this piece of writing?

3. Why do you think Desowitz wrote this?

4. How do the diagrams help you understand the reading?

Getting Ready to Read

The next reading focuses on the global impact of malaria—that is, the effect malaria has on nations. It seeks to inform the reader about the problem and the efforts to control the disease.

Vocabulary Check

These words are in the reading. How many do you know? Check them. Discuss the words with a classmate, and explain any that you know that your partner does not. Then write a definition or an example sentence in your Vocabulary Log.

> Scientists have linked malaria, dengue, and yellow fever to global warming.

_____ consensus   _____ imminent   _____ resurgence

_____ eradication   _____ infrastructure   _____ unprecedented

_____ feasibility   _____ lull (verb)   _____ watershed

_____ genocide   _____ pesticides

_____ groundswell   _____ pharmaceutical

Read

Reading 2: Time to Put Malaria Control on the Global Agenda

by Declan Butler

1 Growing international awareness of the impact of malaria, and in particular the prospect of an **imminent** catastrophe in Africa, is generating an unprecedented **groundswell** for a bold new effort in control.

2   Exactly 100 years after Ronald Ross discovered the role of the mosquito in the life cycle of the malaria parasite, efforts to control the disease stand at what could prove to be a historic **watershed**. Over the past year, a number of research organizations, led by the U.S. National Institutes of Health (NIH) and France's _Institut Pasteur_, have been meeting with malaria researchers, research

The World Health Organization (WHO) was formed in 1946 by the International Health Conference.

charities and development agencies to draw up a coordinated international strategy for malaria research.

3   The outcome of these discussions is being fed into talks between the World Bank and the African office of the World Health Organization (WHO), which are exploring the **feasibility** of setting up a multi-agency, 30-year control program—the African Malaria Initiative. All of these players are in turn talking with the **pharmaceutical** industry to find ways to reverse its **unprecedented** withdrawal from vaccine research and development of antimalarial drugs. Testifying to this movement, this week's *Nature*[1] carries an appeal calling on the international community to mobilize in the fight against malaria (see *Nature*, 386, 541; 1997).

Africa's Cry for Help

4   The impending crisis in Africa has triggered this **resurgence** of interest. The parasite's resistance to chloroquine, the main means of prophylaxis[2] and treatment on the continent, is growing alarmingly.

[1]***Nature:*** a respected scientific journal.

[2]**prophylaxis:** prevention.

Fansidar, the only cheap alternative, seems doomed to the same fate. "It's going to be pretty shocking," predicts Louis Miller, head of the Laboratory of Parasitic Diseases at the U.S. National Institute of Allergy and Infectious Diseases.

5   A recent seven-fold increase in malaria deaths over five years in parts of Senegal has been linked to emergence of chloroquine resistance, according to Jean-François Barakamfityé, a Dakar-based researcher from ORSTOM, the French development research agency. And chloroquine resistance in Senegal is much less intense than in other parts of Africa.

6   Malaria is already estimated to kill between 1.5 and 2.7 million people every year—several times as many as died in the recent **genocide** in Rwanda. Another 300 to 500 million people have the disease, and one-third of all humanity lives in zones where they risk catching it. Malaria kills one person—often a child under five—every 12 seconds.

7   Nine out of ten cases occur in sub-Saharan[3] Africa, and two-thirds of the rest are concentrated in just six countries. These are, in decreasing order of prevalence, India, Brazil, Sri Lanka, Vietnam, Colombia and the Solomon Islands.

8   Malaria is resurging in many countries where it had been eliminated or sharply reduced during the 1950s by a WHO-coordinated campaign to eradicate the vector,[4] Anopheles mosquitoes, using **pesticides** such as DDT.

9   Malaria research and control slipped off the international agenda in the two subsequent decades, says Anatoli Kondrachine, head of malaria control at WHO. The relative success of the campaign **lulled** many countries into a false sense of security, he says. "Now we are paying a very heavy price for that gap."

10   Research is helping to fill that gap. New control measures and treatments are most needed in sub-Saharan Africa, where transmission rates are so high that levels of reduction that would bring the disease to a dead stop in India or Brazil have little impact on mortality. The region was in fact left out of the early **eradication** campaigns precisely for this reason.

11   Outside Africa, much can be done using existing control techniques given adequate commitment. But research is needed to deploy these measures more effectively, and to develop the new tools needed for comprehensive control. Mosquitoes have grown resistant to pesticides, and the harm that these cause to the environment has restricted their use further. New drugs, and the elu-

[3]**sub-Saharan:** the part of Africa below the Sahara. Sub-Saharan Africa is known more for its jungles and wildlife than the northern part of the continent is.

[4]**vector:** in medicine and biology an organism, especially an insect, that carries a disease or parasite from one animal or plant to another.

sive vaccine, are also needed by all malarious countries, not to mention the tourists and other travelers who visit them.

Thirty-Year Offensive
. . . .

12 Faced with this situation, Ebrahim Samba, African regional direc-tor of WHO and Richard Feachem, director for health, nutrition and population at the World Bank—and former dean of the Lon-don School of Hygiene and Tropical Medicine—last year began exploring the idea of creating a multi-agency, 30-year program to control malaria.

13   Discussions have since been broadened to include the U.S. Agency for International Development, U.S. Centers for Disease Control, European Commission, the Organization of African Unity and other agencies. "There should be no delusion that this is a five- or ten-year program," says Feachem. "We are thinking of a 30-year effort, and everyone would need to buy in for durations of that order." Over the past decade, countless international and national strategies to "end malaria" have been devised. But many have gathered dust in government drawers, and few have been properly or fully implemented. "The problem is what people are doing in the field, which is not a lot and not very effectively," com-plains Feachem. The thrust of the new initiative is on building the **infrastructure** needed for malaria control in Africa. Back this with a coordinated and adequately funded international effort, and you have the makings of a situation where existing control and therapeutic tools could be used more effectively, says Feachem. But research would also be an essential component, and the world's major research bodies would therefore need to be "formal partners." Harold Varmus, director of the U.S. National Institutes of Health, says that joining forces would be "very, very healthy for malaria research in Africa." The possibility that the program would fund research directly has not been excluded, says Feachem. "Everything is on the drawing board. The initiative will be an um-brella for many things, and one will need to be a well-directed, adequately funded program of research; it could be inside or out-side, but strongly linked."

14   None of the agencies discussing the proposed African Malaria Initiative is yet talking dollars. But many of those involved are convinced that the program will provide a vehicle for better use of existing funds, and act as a magnet to attract new money from the international community. The initiative has only become possible because of a recent shift in policy at the World Bank. Its support for health projects has leapt from negligible levels in the 1980s to $2 billion annually—about 10 percent of the bank's current spending—and is growing. There is said to be **consensus**

within the bank that, among the problems that Africa faces, malaria is near the top.

Political Support Crucial

15 A decision on whether to launch the African Malaria Initiative is expected later this year, although it would probably not begin until around 2000. "We are in no hurry, we want to get it right," says Feachem.

16   Political and financial commitment from African leaders is acknowledged to be a prerequisite for the success of the initiative. Its supporters argue that there is no point in external agencies putting money into a sector to which the government of the country is not giving priority.

17   In practice, health, and malaria in particular, comes near the bottom of the spending priorities of most African countries, and far behind items such as arms, which often eat as much as half of state spending. But change is in the air. When the Organization of African Unity (OAU) meets for its annual summit later this year, malaria will be on the agenda of the 53 heads of state for the first time.

18   Robert Mshana, executive secretary of the OAU, says that the aim of the summit is to persuade African heads of state to "accept that the [success of the] fight against malaria will be largely dependent on African countries themselves." He adds: "African leaders need to say: 'Malaria is killing our children, we must be determined to do something about it.'"

19   Winning a political commitment would strengthen the hands of health ministers in negotiations with their finance ministries. "We want them to persuade politicians that there are tools which could reduce mortality, that there are considerable economic losses, and that they must allocate the human and financial resources needed," says Barakamfityé.

20   But Mshana also warns that political will is by itself insufficient. "We have had these slogans for the last 50 years and nothing has moved." Governments could help immediately simply by reducing taxes on products used in research, control or therapy, he says: "In some places the import taxes on mosquito nets are so high that nobody can afford them."

◆ After You Read

About the Content

1. What are WHO, NIH, and OAU?

2. Who was Ronald Ross? What did he do?

3. What is the purpose of the African Malaria Initiative?

4. Which countries are most severely affected by malaria?

5. What is chloroquine?

6. About how many people die of malaria each year?

7. What influence do governments have on the control of malaria, according to Butler?

About the Writing

1. What is Butler's main purpose in writing this article?

2. Who do you think the audience for this article is? Why do you think this?

3. There is a lot of difficult vocabulary in this reading. Why do you think the author chose to use this vocabulary?

Analyzing Informative Writing

Although we have defined informative writing as writing that tries to relate information, in fact it often does more than that. In "Time to Put Malaria Control on the Global Agenda," the author's purpose is different than the author's purpose in "The Malaria Capers."

Look over your notes and reread these selections, then answer the following questions with a group of classmates:

1. Why do you think Declan Butler wrote "Time to Put Malaria Control on the Global Agenda"?

2. Why do you think Robert S. Desowitz wrote "The Malaria Capers"?

3. How is the second reading different from the first? Be specific.

4. How do the facts that are presented in the first reading relate to the second?

5. What is your opinion of these readings? Did they interest you?

6. Did you learn new facts and ideas about malaria?

7. Did the authors seem knowledgeable about their subject matter? In what ways?

8. What were the authors' main purposes in writing these articles? How do they accomplish that purpose?

FROM READING TO WRITING

You have read two different types of informative writing. Although both deal with the subject matter of malaria, they approach it in different ways. One is concerned with the social and political issues associated with malaria and its spread, the other with the scientific explanation.

In your essay, you will write about a disease that interests you. You will also have to decide what type of informative writing you will do and what aspect of the disease will be your focus.

◈ **Getting Ready to Write**

For this essay, you will investigate a major disease of interest to you. You may investigate malaria further, or choose another illness to research.

There will be checklists throughout this section to help you fulfill the assignment. Fill in the due dates assigned by your instructor.

Phase 1: Choosing a Topic

When choosing a topic, be sure to choose a subject area that interests you. Here are some ways to help you identify a topic:

1. Brainstorm a list of diseases that have had an effect on you, your family, or your friends. Perhaps your grandfather suffered from diabetes, or your friend's mother has breast cancer. Think of the people around you and the illnesses that affect them.

2. In your journal, quickwrite for 15 minutes, focusing on one of the diseases from your list. Discuss how it affected you or someone you know.

3. Reread your quickwrite. Identify sentences or passages that you think are well-written, or that you would like to expand upon. Highlight or underline these sections.

4. On a new piece of paper, develop those passages into an essay of one or two pages. In this essay, you will state the disease you chose and explain why you chose it. Give specific examples of why this disease is important or interesting to you. This short essay will become the introduction to your longer research paper, which you will write in the next chapter.

TUNING IN: "Panic Disorder"

Watch the CNN video on "Panic Disorder." Discuss these questions with your classmates:

© CNN

1. What is a panic attack?

2. What are some symptoms of a panic attack?

3. Who is most likely to suffer panic disorder?

4. How is panic disorder treated?

In your journal, respond to these questions: Does anything make you panic? What? How do you deal with the feeling of panic?

Phase 2: Beginning Your Research

You need to be sure that your subject is possible to research. Although the discovery of a new virus reported in this morning's newspaper may be fascinating, you might have difficulty finding much information on such a recent finding. To ensure that there is adequate information, go to your library to do preliminary research.

When you have chosen a topic and done some preliminary research, fill out Checklist 1.

Due Date: _____/_____/_____

Checklist 1. Topic of Interest _____

_____ The topic fulfills the assignment.

_____ There is adequate information on this topic.

_____ My instructor has approved my choice.

> A man's health can be judged by which he takes two at a time— pills or stairs.
>
> —JOAN WELSH

Defining Your Approach

The *approach* you take in writing is your unique way of looking at a topic. In the readings in the chapter, Butler's approach is to discuss the battle to end malaria and its obstacles. Desowitz's approach focuses on the details of the transmission of the disease through mosquitoes.

In your essay, for example, you might choose to research AIDS as a subject. There are many different approaches to this topic: the scientific explanation, the disease's social impact, prevention, the research that discovered the disease, and so on. As you narrow the focus of your subject, there are three principles to consider in choosing an approach:

- **Completeness.** When you choose your approach, make sure you can cover it well. Make your approach specific and manageable. For example, if you want to discuss the history of a disease, you may not be able to cover all the important ideas in a six-page paper.

- **Surprise value.** In your approach, find something interesting to say. In other words, your approach should reflect your own interests and point of view. Don't just summarize the information you find.

- **Factuality**. As the writer of information, you are responsible for providing an accurate piece of writing that correctly and fully documents sources and facts.

These three factors are not completely separate. With each principle you focus on, you will probably be doing (or at least thinking about) the other parts of the task. When you have decided on your approach, complete Checklist 2.

Due Date: _____/_____/_____

Checklist 2. Approach

The approach I want to take to my subject is _____

_____.

I've discussed this approach with my classmates or my instructor. _____

Write one paragraph that explains your approach: _____

_____

_____

_____

Read your approach to a partner. Answer any questions he or she might have about it. Your partner will read you his or her approach as well. Ask questions about anything that isn't clear to you. Before you go the library or the Internet to begin more serious research, take a few minutes to freewrite or map out what you already know about your subject matter. Use this time to formulate questions and jot down ideas.

From your prewriting and reading notes, identify as many **keywords** as you can to help you with your research. For example, if malaria prevention interests you, the keywords *DDT* and *chloroquine* will be useful.

ACADEMIC POWER STRATEGY

Familiarize yourself with what is in your library to do research more efficiently in all your classes. Whether you use a small local library or a large university library, it is important to take some time to explore the place where you will be doing research.

Apply the Strategy

1. Find out if the librarians offer tours. You can learn about resources such as computer indexes, microfilm, photocopiers, video libraries, and any other specialty items by touring the library with someone who works there.

2. Spend time looking around. Find and explore the reference room, and the magazines and newspapers kept there. Walk through each floor. Learn where the books related to your classes and interests are found.

3. List the card catalogues or computer programs that are available in your library:

   _____

   _____

4. Use *Readers' Guide* and newspaper indexes to find articles that appear in magazines and newspapers. For back issues, your library probably has newspapers on microfilm or microfiche.

5. In your library, where can you find a) *Readers' Guide*, b) newspaper indexes, and c) newspapers on microfilm or microfiche?

6. Use computer databases and CD-ROMs to find current articles in specific areas.

Library Searches

If you have never searched for information in your library, you should ask the reference librarian for assistance. Reference librarians are experts at finding information and can help you start an efficient search. Use the card catalogue or computer search program to look up the disease you chose. Then check to see what is actually available in your library.

LANGUAGE LEARNING STRATEGY

Use library resources to make your essays stronger and more informative. After you have learned how to use your library, it is important to start using the materials you find there to support your ideas. Using resources will help you to learn more and to share more information with your readers.

(continued on next page)

Apply the Strategy

1. Use the information you have learned about your library to begin putting together resources for your essay. Begin with your library's computer or card catalogue. Do a "subject" search, using your keywords. Some library systems list books only, others have computer databases that list articles as well. List three sources that look promising to you:

   _____

   _____

2. Find one of the sources you identified. Check it out of the library if it's a book; photocopy it if it's an article. If you photocopy your sources, be sure to write the full reference of your article somewhere on the copy (author, title, publisher, city, date, and page numbers). It is also helpful to write the call number (the library identification number that tells where the book can be found) of the book or journal you took the copy from so that you can return to it easily if necessary.

3. At the end of most articles and books, you will find a bibliography of the sources the author used. Look them over to see if there is something that would be useful to your own research. If so, check to see if this source is available in your library.

Internet Searches

Of course, you can use the Internet as a library of information, too. Learn to use search engines or other tools to help you with your research.

In the next chapter, you will organize your research, evaluate your sources, and write your research paper.

Write

Now that you have located your resources, be sure that you keep copies of those that are interesting and important to you. Review all of your quickwrites, notes, and readings. Now, write a two- to three-page essay in which you explain your interest in the disease you have chosen. This essay will serve as an introduction to the research writing you will do in the next chapter.

After You Write

Revise

Give your draft to a classmate. Ask your reader for specific feedback on the process you describe. Ask your partner to answer these questions:

1. Has the writer chosen an interesting subject?

2. Is the writer's interest in the subject matter clear?

3. Has the writer included any sources?

4. What other comments do you have for the writer?

Now complete the table below, as you did in the previous chapter. Use your revision plan to guide your rewriting.

Feature	Problem	Possible Solution
Title		
Opening paragraph		
Logical ordering (clear plan)		
Word choice		
Conclusion		
Other		

(Also, refer to page 38 of Chapter 2 for help in revising your draft.)

Grammar You Can Use: Prepositions

There are so many prepositions and combinations of words with prepositions that it is impossible to cover them all here. There are no rules to refer to, and many uses are idiomatic, or even vary regionally (for example, in New York City you might stand *on* line, but in California you stand *in* line).

Although there are no real "rules" for prepositions, there is a "system." This system reflects the way we look at objects in the world. Think about the following pair of examples:

Angel got *on* the bus.   Ali got *in* my car.

In both cases, people enter types of transportation—why is one in and one on? Look at another pair of examples:

Juan is *in* the corner.   Marla is *at* the corner.

Which person is more likely to be outdoors?

These examples show that prepositions relate to the way we see places and surfaces. In the first pair of examples, Angel got *on* a bus because she can walk *on* its floor, or move around *on* it. The same applies to airplanes and trains. However, a car is a "container"—it's difficult to walk *on* the car unless you are *on* the outside of it. Therefore, we get *in* our cars.

In the second instance, Marla is most likely to be outdoors. Juan is inside the two walls that form a corner, so he is probably *in* a room. Marla is *at* the outer point where two walls meet, so she is probably outside. This can be seen in the simple drawing below:

"in" vs. "at" the corner

Many prepositions are used in **phrasal verbs**—that is, a verb and a preposition-like word (called a "particle") combination that has a unique meaning, different from that of the verb, and often not predictable from the meaning of the two words themselves.

With true phrasal verbs (where the preposition functions as a particle), you can use two different word orders:

I *looked up* the word in the dictionary.

I *looked* the word *up* in the dictionary.

You cannot do this if the preposition is simply a preposition and not a particle:

Correct: I *looked up* at the airplane.

Incorrect: I *looked* at the airplane *up*.

In your journal or notebook, keep track of phrasal verbs or uses of prepositions you have trouble with, along with their meanings or examples. If your instructor has marked an incorrect preposition in your writing, ask for an explanation if you don't understand it. Rewrite the correct phrase.

Practice with Prepositions

Insert a correct preposition in each blank. Different answers may be possible.

1. Americans are probably the most pain-conscious people _____ the face _____ the earth. _____ years we have had it drummed _____ us—_____ print, _____ radio, _____ television,

_____ everyday conversation—that any hint _____ pain is to be banished as though it were the ultimate evil."

—Norman Cousins

2. We got our TV set _____ 1959, when I was 5. So I can barely remember life without television. I have spent 20,000 hours _____ my life _____ front _____ the set. Not all _____ my contemporaries watched so much, but many did, and what's more, we watched the same programs, heard the same commercials, were exposed _____ the same end-_____-show lessons.

—Joyce Maynard

3. As I write this, _____ an airplane, I have run _____ _____ paper and need to reach _____ my briefcase _____ my legs _____ more. I cannot do this until my empty lunch tray is removed _____ my lap.

—William F. Buckley, Jr.

4. _____ me the most interesting thing _____ a solitary life, and mine has been that _____ the last twenty years, is that it becomes increasingly rewarding. When I can wake _____ and watch the sun rise _____ the ocean, as I do most days, and know that I have an entire day ahead, uninterrupted, _____ which to write a few pages, take a walk _____ my dog, lie down _____ the afternoon _____ a long think (why does one think better _____ a horizontal position?), read and listen _____ music, I am flooded _____ happiness.

—May Sarton

5. A broad expanse _____ the river was turned _____ blood; the middle distance the red hue brightened _____ gold, _____ which a solitary log came floating black and conspicuous; _____ one place a long slanting mark lay sparkling _____ the

water; _____ another the surface was broken _____ boiling, tumbling rings, that were as many tinted as an opal. . . .

—Mark Twain

Self-Correction

In your essay assignment, identify areas where you had difficulty with prepositions. Copy any sentences with preposition errors in them; then rewrite each sentence correctly.

Edit

After you have solved the problems identified in your revision plan, you can focus on editing and proofreading your paper. The editing phase includes double-checking your grammar, spelling, punctuation, and so forth. Each student has unique problems in this area, so it may be helpful to take an inventory of problem spots, based on your past experience as a writer. Remember, you can change this inventory as you progress.

Which of the following items do you think are a problem for you? Check the appropriate column.

PROBLEM	MAJOR PROBLEM	MINOR PROBLEM	NO PROBLEM	DON'T KNOW
Spelling	_____	_____	_____	_____
Punctuation	_____	_____	_____	_____
Subject–verb agreement	_____	_____	_____	_____
Verb tenses	_____	_____	_____	_____
Articles	_____	_____	_____	_____
Prepositions	_____	_____	_____	_____
Plurals	_____	_____	_____	_____
Sentence fragments	_____	_____	_____	_____
Run-on sentences	_____	_____	_____	_____
Wordiness	_____	_____	_____	_____
Parallel structures	_____	_____	_____	_____

If you have checked more than three as a "major problem," decide which three you would like to work on first. It's easier to concentrate on a few problem areas at a time.

The last step should be proofreading—that is, looking for careless mistakes: misspellings, leaving out words, typing words twice in a row, and so forth. Before you turn your paper in, proofread it carefully.

Test-Taking Tip

Underline key words in test essay questions. Examples of key words are: *compare, explain, justify,* and *define*. These words tell you what approach to take in answering the question. Underlining these words will help you understand and focus on what you are being asked. It will also ensure that you answer precisely what is being asked, without writing off the topic.

CHECK YOUR PROGRESS

As you did in previous chapters, on a scale of 1 to 5, rate how well you have mastered the goals set at the beginning of the chapter:

1 2 3 4 5 think about your purpose for writing in order to write in a more focused way.

1 2 3 4 5 familiarize yourself with what is in your library to do research more efficiently.

1 2 3 4 5 use library resources to make your essays stronger and more informative.

1 2 3 4 5 use prepositions correctly.

1 2 3 4 5 (your own goal) _____

1 2 3 4 5 (your own goal) _____

If you've given yourself a 3 or lower on any of these goals:

- visit the *Tapestry* web site for additional practice.
- ask your instructor for extra help.
- review the sections of the chapter that you found difficult.
- work with a partner or study group to further your progress.

PUTTING IT ALL TOGETHER

This word-search puzzle contains some of the vocabulary you learned in this chapter. Locate the words, which go in any direction. Cross them off the list as you find them. The first one is done for you.

```
L  A  C  I  T  U  E  C  A  M  R  A  H  P
R  B  E  C  N  E  G  R  U  S  E  R  X  E
U  N  P  R  E  C  E  D  E  N  T  E  D  R
E  Y  U  P  R  M  G  C  P  E  M  K  Z  U
L  Y  Q  U  A  M  E  L  T  I  B  C  V  T
B  V  O  S  D  R  A  B  A  S  E  I  M  C
I  Q  W  M  I  E  A  B  Y  N  Y  R  I  U
S  E  D  I  C  I  T  S  E  P  D  C  M  R
A  D  B  U  A  D  K  H  I  O  M  U  M  T
E  A (M  A  T  R  I  X) E  T  M  L  I  S
F  I  E  D  I  C  O  N  E  G  E  A  N  A
E  R  P  R  O  L  I  F  E  R  A  T  E  R
E  Y  C  O  N  S  E  N  S  U  S  O  N  F
I  M  U  E  T  A  C  I  L  P  E  R  T  N
C  H  E  M  O  T  H  E  R  A  P  Y  S  I
```

AMOEBA	PARASITE	IMMINENT	CHEMOTHERAPY
PROLIFERATE	INFRASTRUCTURE	CIRCULATORY	FEASIBILE
CYST	REPLICATE	PESTICIDES	RESURGENCE
GLAND	CONSENSUS	PHARMACEUTICAL	ERADICATION
~~MATRIX~~	MYRIAD	GENOCIDE	UNPRECEDENTED

L ook closely at the photos, and then discuss these questions with your classmates:

- Which of these people is doing research?
- What kind of research have you done before?
- Why is it important to use research in academic writing?

7

RESEARCHING: GETTING TO THE SOURCE

In the previous chapter, you began the process of doing research. In this chapter, you will put the different pieces of your work together into your research paper. In particular, you will learn some of the techniques of quoting sources effectively and making sure that the research you do is original and interesting.

Setting Goals

This chapter will provide you with some strategies and techniques for writing researched essays. You will learn how to:

◈ avoid plagiarism in all of your writing.

◈ write effective conclusions.

◈ develop a clear point of view in your research writing.

◈ use quotations effectively and correctly.

What other goals do you have for learning about writing research papers? Write two more here.

_____

_____

◆**Getting Started**

Before you begin the chapter, take a few minutes to write down what you know about writing a research paper. You can begin by answering these questions:

- Why is it important to use outside sources for your writing?
- Why are quotations used in researched writing?
- What is plagiarism?

TUNING IN: "Boston University Plagiarism"

© CNN

Watch the CNN video about plagiarism at Boston University. Discuss these questions with your class:

- Who is Joachim Maitre?
- Why was he asked to resign from his position at Boston University?
- Do you believe Maitre's explanation that he forgot to include an attribution to Medvel?
- How did the Boston University students react?

In your journal, respond to this question:

How would you feel if you discovered that someone had turned in something you wrote for their own school assignment? What would you do?

◆**Getting Ready to Read**

The following reading focuses on defining what a research paper is. Watch the CNN video and discuss it before you go through the next reading.

◆**Vocabulary Check**

These words are in the reading. Check the words you know. Discuss the words you don't know with a classmate. Use a dictionary, if necessary. Then write a definition or an example sentence in your Vocabulary Log.

_____ constitute	_____ indefensible	_____ synthesis
_____ conventions	_____ plagiarism	_____ unsubstantiated
_____ endeavor		

Reading 1: What Is a Research Paper?

by Audrey J. Roth

What a Research Paper Is

1   A research paper is an entirely new work, one you create, one that can only be found on the pages you write. It will have a number of qualities that reflect you, that make it your own special creation.

1. The research paper synthesizes your discoveries about a topic and your judgment, interpretation, and evaluation of those discoveries.

2   Your discoveries consist mostly of the ideas, knowledge, and actual words of people who have written, spoken, or made pictures about the subject you investigated. They are likely to come from both print and nonprint sources. But all that collected material only has value because you weighed your discoveries and drew conclusions from them. Your involvement is evident because the entire research paper reflects your own ideas as much as those of anyone else who has worked on the subject.

3   Selecting information to use is a personal process. Deciding how to approach this information, developing a point of view toward it, and, finally, choosing your own words to present it are all highly personal activities. Therefore, the more you involve yourself in these activities, the more the resulting research paper will be your own!

2. The research paper is a work that shows your originality.

4   The paper resulting from your study, evaluation, and **synthesis** will be a totally new creation, something you originate. True, you will have put many hours of thought and much effort into a work that takes only a short time to read. But that is the nature of any creative **endeavor.**

Moreover, it's a real art to make the difficult appear easy, not to let an audience be aware of preparation and practice. What you read most easily is often a result of the most work. In a carefully crafted research paper, your own hand and thought—your originality—are evident.

3. The research paper acknowledges all sources you used.

5   Documentation and acknowledgment of what is not original is so basic to research papers that a whole series of customs or **conventions** has developed for crediting what you borrow from other people.[1]

6   Ethical behavior also demands that you acknowledge the sources that contributed to your work. Finding information and making it available to others, whether in writing, orally, or in film, is hard work. Just as you do these tasks for a research paper, so others have done the same (or similar) tasks for what became your sources. So although your research paper is a new and original work, none of it would have been possible without the various sources you consulted to prepare it. Acknowledging that debt to others is only right and fair!

What a Research Paper Is Not

7   If you accept the definition that a research paper is a synthesis of your thought applied to the material supplied to you by others, that it is original, and that it acknowledges source material—you will never make the mistake of attempting to hand in what is certainly not a research paper.

1. A summary of an article or a book (or other source material) is NOT a research paper.

---

[1]Appendix 2 shows you how to document your work in MLA and APA formats.

8   A summary can't fit our definition of a re-search paper for two reasons: 1) a single source doesn't allow you to select materials or to exercise your own judgment and 2) the organization can't be your own because a summary must follow the structure of the original source.

9   Summaries of written, visual, or audio materials have their uses—and they are important ones—but substituting for a research paper is not one of them.

2. The ideas of others, repeated uncritically, do NOT make a research paper.

10   By definition, the research paper has to reflect something about yourself—a synthesis, an interpretation, or some other personal involvement. To repeat, uncritically, what others have said is merely to report information already available elsewhere. For example, no amount of reading about a novel can substitute for reading the work yourself, any more than reading about a musical group can substitute for hearing the musicians perform.

3. A series of quotations, no matter how skillfully put together, does NOT make a research paper.

11   Quotations have an important place in a research paper because they are the words of experts in the field—or of those who are experts with words. But if your paper is nothing more than a series of quotations, the "you" of the synthesis is missing; you, yourself, are not involved in such a paper, and the work certainly gives no evidence of your originality.

12   Furthermore, each quotation is likely to have an individual style. To organize dozens of quotations from different people into a coherent whole is impossible!

4. Unsubstantiated personal opinion does NOT constitute a research paper.

13   Individual beliefs and attitudes are valuable in certain kinds of writing assignments, but the research paper is not one of them. For one thing, the "search" aspect is entirely lacking. For another, the research paper topic is not one that lends itself to opinions without extensive and factual bases.

5. Copying or accepting another person's work without acknowledging it, whether the work is published or unpublished, professional or amateur is NOT research. IT IS PLAGIARISM.

14   It is morally wrong to pass off as your own any writing you did not do. To present such work without acknowledging the source—and therefore let someone assume it is yours when, in fact, it is not—is plagiarism. Turning in as your own a research paper done by someone else is indefensible, whether you accept it from a friend trying to help you out or you bought it from a company that supplies research papers. There are laws against plagiarism, and in many schools any student involved in plagiarism (including the supplier of such a paper) is automatically dismissed.

15   On the most literal level, perhaps no word or thought is completely original; you learned it somewhere. Often only the finest line of distinction separates what must be credited in a research paper from what you can safely present without documentation.

16   Students who respect themselves and their work will certainly not be tempted to copy from anyone. Instead, they will always extend proper credit for others, as well as for specific wording.

◆**After You Read**

About the Content

1. In what ways does a research paper reflect its writer?

2. In what ways is selecting information a "personal process," according to the author?

3. Why isn't a summary a research paper?

4. Why is it important to critically analyze your sources?

5. How should quotations be used in order to be effective?

About the Writing

1. How is this paper organized?

2. Is this an effective organization technique?

3. Do you find the tone of this writing effective? How would you describe it?

ACADEMIC POWER STRATEGY

Avoid plagiarism in all of your writing. The previous reading points out the ethical problems with copying others' work. However, plagiarism is a more complex issue than just copying. For example, imagine that you read a book that argued that Africans were the first explorers to land in North America, not the Vikings or Columbus. The argument you read made a lot of sense, and you agreed with it. Can you write a paper in which you talk about *your* theory of Africans landing in North America? In short, no. This is plagiarism, because the theory is someone else's. You can write about this theory, but you must credit the original source of the idea in your writing.

What if you know that Columbus first landed in North America on October 12, 1492? You don't know where you read this; you probably learned it in elementary school, in fact. Do you need to cite the source of this knowledge? The answer is no. This is what is called *common knowledge*. In other words, it is a fact that any reasonably educated person is expected to know, so you need not state a specific source.

The line between common knowledge and ideas you must quote can be blurry, however. If you have any question at all about the source of information, you should ask your instructor, or give a source. Always err on the side of being too cautious rather than not cautious enough when it comes to citing your sources.

Apply the Strategy

Find out what your school's policy is on plagiarism. Find the official rules, and share them with your class. Discuss how you can avoid plagiarism and why you should avoid it.

Writing Tip: Using Your Sources

In Chapter 6, you began to gather sources for your paper. In this section, you will learn to incorporate those sources into your paper. There are four ways of incorporating outside material into your own writing:

1. Paraphrases introduce the same information, but completely in your own words.

2. Direct quotations are pieces of the text used because they report information in a unique or particularly interesting way.

3. If direct quotations are longer than three lines, you should use block quotations. These are indented and set off from the rest of the text.

4. A brief summary gives a quick overview, again in your own words, of the main ideas of a passage

> The best way to become acquainted with a subject is to write a book about it
>
> —BENJAMIN DISRAELI

Imagine you are writing your research paper about the discovery of the HIV virus. You want to use information from *And the Band Played On*, by Randy Shilts. The following passage is taken from that book. Read the passage; then use the activity following the passage to practice each of the types of quotation above.

> By now, a dizzying array of acronyms was being bandied about as possible monikers for an epidemic that, though ten months old, remained unnamed. Besides GRID, some doctors liked ACIDS, for Acquired Community Immune Deficiency Syndrome, and then others favored CAIDS, for Community Acquired Immune Deficiency Syndrome. The CDC hated GRID and preferred calling it "the epidemic of immune deficiency." The "community" in other versions, of course, was a polite way of saying gay; the doctors couldn't let go of the notion that one identified this disease by whom it hit rather than what it did.
>
> Whether CAIDS, ACIDS, or GRID, the epidemic had by April 2, 1982, struck 300 Americans and killed 119. In the past two weeks, cases had been detected in two more states and two more European nations, indicating that the epidemic had now spread across nineteen states and seven countries.

1. Paraphrase the first two sentences: _____

_____

_____

2. Write a direct quotation from the first paragraph (include the author's name and book title in introducing the quotation):

3. Write a block quotation from the second paragraph (include the author's name and book title in introducing the quotation):

4. Summarize the passage using your own words: _____

The largest public library in the United States is the Los Angeles Public Library system, which serves more than 6 million people and has more than 11 million books.

Writing Tip: Punctuating Quotations

When you use sources, you need to use quotations. Here are the ways in which you should punctuate them.

Type of Quoted Material	Explanation	Example
Direct quotation	Use quotation marks, introduced by a comma or colon.	According to the author, "Bioengineering is a growing field." The researchers concluded: "Bioengineering is a growing field."
Quoted words or phrases	Do not use a comma or colon.	The writers considered the event an "end of an era."
Quotation within a quotation	Use single quotation marks when someone you quote is quoting someone else.	The author states: "Many researchers cut corners, and according to Dr. M.E. Marshall, 'don't care about the consequences.'"
Excerpted quotation	Use an ellipsis—three spaced periods—to show that you have shortened a quotation by leaving out some words. If you omit material at the end of a sentence, you will use four periods.	According to the authors, "Many jobs will be lost . . . with increased automation." They go on to say that "this is not necessarily a bad thing . . . ."
Additions to quotations	If you add information to a quotation in order to clarify it, use square brackets to show your additions.	In their report, Drs. Jones and Hidalgo state, "The beginning of the year [1999] will find even more inventions on the landscape."

Getting Ready to Read

The next reading is a sample research paper that looks at myths about curing the common cold. Do you think it's important to find a cure? Why or why not? Discuss this with your class.

As you read the paper, read the notes about it also, which explain the different parts of the paper. Note that this paper uses APA (American Psychological Association) format (see Appendix 2, page 214). This is a common format for citing work.

Vocabulary Check

The words in this list are included in the reading. Check the ones that you know. Look up the ones you don't, or discuss them with a classmate. Then write a definition or an example sentence in your Vocabulary Log.

_____ eradicate   _____ induce

_____ foresee   _____ predicament

_____ hydration   _____ salivation

Read

Give your paper a descriptive title.

Introduce your reader to the general topic of your paper in your introduction.

Be sure to include a thesis or main point in your introduction. It is underlined here.

Introduce your information by stating clearly its source and authors.

This information is paraphrased. That is, it is in the author's own words, though the information came from her research.

This is a direct quotation. They are the exact words spoken by Professor Eccles.

Be sure to indicate the page number of quotations.

Reading 2: Are There Cures for the Common Cold?

1   People often face the **predicament** of catching the "common cold" and not knowing what to do to feel better. Some people say that rest is the best medicine, while others say "Feed a fever and starve a cold." It seems that many myths exist about how to cure this virus. <u>However, it is not always clear what is fact and what is myth when talking about the common cold.</u>

2   According to Jones, Nakashima, and Franco, in their article "Colds and How They Happen" (1998), there are approximately 200 viruses that cause the common cold. These viruses can survive for several hours on hands, clothing, and hard surfaces, such as door knobs or sinks. The cold is the most common disease among humans: every day, about 50 million people around the globe wake up with one.

3   After many years of research, the head of the Common Cold Center in Wales has reached a conclusion. Unfortunately, there is no cure for the common cold. Professor Ron Eccles, the director of the center at University of Wales, Cardiff, says: "I don't **foresee** a cure in which we **eradicate** all the viruses. I think the best we can hope for is to live at peace with it" (1998, p. 2).

4   But how do we live in peace with this virus? In spite of there being no cure, there are many myths about treatment. Or are they myths?

5   The most common myths about treating a cold is that colds can be cured by drinking lots of orange juice (for the vitamin C it contains) and eating chicken soup.

5   Dr. Daniel Danali, a family physician and professor of medicine, writes in his book *Common Colds: Myths and Sad Realities*, "Most of these myths are not completely true. There are no studies showing that any vitamins or chicken soup will cure the common cold" (1997, p. 44). He also says that orange juice, tea, and chicken soup do not make colds go away. "You would have to drink two gallons of orange juice to get enough vitamin C to begin to fight the cold virus," he says (1997, pp. 99–100).

When a quotation goes over more than one page, write "pp." (meaning "pages").

6   However, another report by Drs. Jill Jobs and Alberto Martinez of the Viral Control Clinic of Chicago, states the following:

> Warm liquids, such as chicken soup or tea, help relieve congestion. They are bland and easy to digest, if the patient has an upset stomach. Juice and tea offer the proper **hydration,** necessary for the body to keep fighting the virus. (1996, p. 16)

This is a block quotation. It is more than three lines, so it is indented and separated from the rest of the text. No quotation marks are put around it.

It appears from this report that part of the myth might in fact be true.

7   The common cold also often comes with an uncomfortable sore throat. (Luckily, the methods to help ease the pain can also taste good.) According to Jobs and Martinez, it is important to keep the sore throat moist. They state, "Sucking on cough drops or candy **induces salivation**." They also say that other alternatives include eating ice cream, yogurt, or honey. The ice cream can cool the burning sensation in the back of the throat that often accompanies a cold or flu (1996, p. 11).

8   It is also common with a cold or flu to experience an upset stomach. According to a University of Springfield report, an upset stomach can be soothed by drinking herbal teas. Teas and herbs decrease cramps by decreasing acid production (1998).

Here the author brings in evidence from another study.

9   The report also states Chinese have included herbs and plants in their medical practices for many years. Many of their recipes include plants such as licorice, ginger, cinnamon and peppermint, which are used to cure anything from headaches or sleeplessness that can come with being ill (1998).

10   Colds can often lead to infections. Surprisingly, teas may also be used in cases of eye infections. It is recommended that a warm tea bag be placed directly on the eye. The tannic acid, the substance that makes the tea brown, helps kill the bacteria (Johnson, 1995, p. 100).

11   The research presented above shows that while many home remedies may not cure the common cold, some of them can help make it less uncomfortable. Rather than dismiss home remedies as useless myths, it is clearly important to investigate the science that might be behind them. After all, hundreds of years of tea and mother's chicken soup can't be all wrong.

This is the author's conclusion. It starts with a brief summary of the research, then shows what the importance of the study is.

Your reference list gives all the information from the items you quoted or referred to. (See page 216 for more information on formatting your references.)

Be sure you use a "hanging indent"[1] on your reference listings.

Your reference listings should be in alphabetical order, by last name of the author.

Include web pages and Internet sources on your reference list, too. Include the complete URL, or address of its location.

References

Danali, D. (1997). *Common colds: Myths and sad realities*. Boston: University Press.

Eccles, R. (1998). Ten years of research on the common cold. University of Wales Press.

Jobs, J., & Martinez, A. (1996) A report on treating the common cold. *General Medicine Newsletter:* 10–18.

Johnson, M. (1995). The many uses of tea. *Science and Nature Magazine,* 55, 99–102.

Jones, T., Nakashima, I., & Franco, D. (1998). Colds and how they happen. *Journal of Virus Science 3,* 45–66.

University of Springfield (1998). A report on cold treatments. URL: http://www.uspringfield.edu/medical/colds.html

After You Read

About the Content

1. What is the main point of this reading?
2. What are some of the myths about the common cold?
3. What are some useful treatments for the common cold?
4. How is tea useful in treating a cold?

> The average person has two colds a year. Their duration is equivalent to having a cold for a total of three years of life.

About the Writing

1. What kinds of information did the author use to prove her claim?
2. Was the author effective in proving her point?
3. What is your opinion of the author's title for the writing? Can you think of a better one?

FROM READING TO WRITING

You have read about doing research and using sources effectively. You have also read an essay about the common cold, that showed the important parts of a research paper. You will apply these research skills and writing techniques in your research paper.

[1] **hanging indent:** the first line is at the left margin, but the following lines of each entry are indented 3–5 spaces. Most word processing programs have a setting for this.

◆ Getting Ready to Write

LANGUAGE LEARNING STRATEGY

Develop a clear point of view in your research writing to make it more interesting. Whether you call it a point of view, a hook, or an attitude, it is important that your research writing clearly tells your point of view about your subject matter. In the paper about colds, the author didn't choose simply to write about "the common cold," but a specific aspect of colds: the usefulness of certain myths about curing colds. Her point of view was to challenge the idea that certain ideas are just "myths," and she looked for research to support that idea.

Apply the Strategy

Review the material you gathered in Chapter 6 for your paper. What point of view will you adopt? Think specifically about what interests you. Brainstorm a list of possible approaches for your topic (see page 4 for a review of brainstorming). A list for the common cold is given as an example.

The Common Cold   **Your topic:** _____

1. Myths and truths: who is right?   1.

2. How it is caught   2.

3. Its effect on productivity in the   3.
   workplace

Write

After you have defined your approach, outline your paper. How many examples will you provide? Do you have the information you need to support those examples? Fill out the information in this chart.

Your main idea: _____

Explain the issue you will explore: _____

_____

_____

Describe the first example you will use to support your idea:

_____

_____

Who will you quote or paraphrase to support this? (If you don't know yet, do more research to find the information you need.)

_____

_____

_____

_____

Describe the next example you will use to support your idea:

_____

_____

_____

_____

Who will you quote or paraphrase to support this? (If you don't know yet, do more research to find the information you need.)

_____

_____

_____

_____

Describe the next example you will use to support your idea:

_____

_____

_____

_____

Who will you quote or paraphrase to support this? (If you don't know yet, do more research to find the information you need.)

_____

_____

_____

_____

(Repeat this step for as many examples as you have.)

How will you conclude your paper? _____

_____

_____

_____

What questions or problems do you still have? _____

_____

_____

_____

Use this outline as a guide to writing your paper.

LANGUAGE LEARNING STRATEGY

Learn to write effective conclusions in order to make your writing more effective. Your conclusion is your last opportunity to make an impression on your reader. What kind of impression will you leave? A good conclusion accomplishes three things: 1) it briefly but effectively emphasizes the main ideas of the paper, 2) it illustrates the importance of the ideas, and 3) it answers the questions posed by the earlier part of the paper.

Apply the Strategy

Review the papers you have written for this class. Look especially at the conclusions. Rewrite any conclusions that don't satisfy the guidelines given here. Share your conclusions with a classmate and discuss how to improve them.

After You Write

After you have finished writing, give your draft to a classmate. Ask your reader for specific feedback on your writing. Ask your partner to answer these questions:

1. Is the main point of the research clear?
2. Is the research clearly documented?
3. Are quotations used properly?
4. Is the research original and interesting?
5. How could the conclusion be improved?

Now complete the following table, as you did in the previous chapter. Use your revision plan to guide your rewriting.

(Also refer to page 38 of Chapter 2 for help in revising your draft.)

Feature	Problem	Possible Solution
Title		
Opening paragraph		
Logical ordering (clear plan)		
Word choice		
Use of quotations		
Conclusion		
Other comments		

Grammar You Can Use: Quotations in Research

The following is an example of a direct quotation:

> Dr. Johnson: "The common cold will last one week if you treat it, or seven days if you don't."

When you are reporting speech, the common way of doing so would be through reported speech:

> Dr. Johnson said that the common cold would last one week if I treated it, or seven days if I didn't.

You can see that in changing a direct quotation to an indirect one, you can add the word *that*, change the pronouns as necessary, and change the verb tense. However, when you are quoting from books, the verb tenses generally do not change. That is, if Dr. Johnson had written the quotation above, you would write the following: Dr. Johnson states that the common cold will last one week if treated, or seven days if untreated.

Practice with these three examples. Change each into an indirect quotation:

1. The report states: "The suggestion now is that prevention is better than an attempt at a cure." _____

   _____

   The researcher asks: "How long does it take an infection to clear without the use of antibiotics?" _____

   _____

Randy Shilts writes: "... The epidemic had by April 2, 1982, struck 300 Americans and killed 119." _____

_____

Self-Correction:

In your essay assignment, identify areas where you had difficulty with direct and indirect quotations. Copy any passages with quotation errors in them, then rewrite each sentence correctly.

Edit

After you have solved the problems identified in your revision plan, you can focus on editing and proofreading your paper. The editing phase includes double-checking your grammar, spelling, punctuation, and so forth. Each student has unique problems in this area, so it may be helpful to take an inventory of problem spots, based on your past experience as a writer. Remember, you can change this inventory as you progress.

Which of the following items do you think are a problem for you? Check the appropriate column.

PROBLEM	MAJOR PROBLEM	MINOR PROBLEM	NO PROBLEM	DON'T KNOW
Spelling	___	___	___	___
Punctuation	___	___	___	___
Subject–verb agreement	___	___	___	___
Verb tenses	___	___	___	___
Articles	___	___	___	___
Prepositions	___	___	___	___
Plurals	___	___	___	___
Sentence fragments	___	___	___	___
Run-on sentences	___	___	___	___
Wordiness	___	___	___	___
Quotation format	___	___	___	___
Clear conclusions	___	___	___	___

If you have checked more than three as a "major problem," decide which three you would like to work on first. It's easier to concentrate on a few problem areas at a time.

The last step should be proofreading—that is, looking for careless mistakes: misspellings, leaving out words, typing words twice in a row, and so forth. Before you turn your paper in, proofread it carefully.

PUTTING IT ALL TOGETHER

◊ **Use What You Have Learned**

Look at your local television listings. Find a program that deals with health or medicine, and watch it. Report on the show you watched to your classmates. You can use the outline provided below.

A. On your own, use the following spaces to take notes as you watch the program on health or medicine.

1. Name of television show watched:

2. Describe the main point of the program: _____

_____

_____

_____

_____

_____

3. What did you learn from this program? _____

_____

_____

_____

_____

_____

B. In class, find a classmate who watched a different program, and complete the questions in this part.

1. Describe to your partner your answer for question 2 in section A. Try to recall all the details you can.

2. Describe your answer to question 3 to your partner. Explain two things you found most interesting about the program, and tell why they were interesting.

Test-Taking Tip

Don't just regret your mistakes on tests, learn from them. You can learn a lot from your mistakes—take advantage of this opportunity.

- Look carefully at the mistake. Don't try to hide it or blame someone else for it.

- Correct the mistake immediately. If you don't know the correct answer, find out.

- Think about why you made the mistake. Did you misunderstand the question? Did you not study hard enough?

- Make an appointment to talk to your instructor about your errors. Show that you care about more than your grade—show you really want to learn the material.

CHECK YOUR PROGRESS

On a scale of 1 to 5, rate how well you have mastered the goals set at the beginning of the chapter:

1 2 3 4 5   avoid plagiarism in all of your writing.

1 2 3 4 5   write effective conclusions.

1 2 3 4 5   develop a clear point of view in your research writing.

1 2 3 4 5   use quotations effectively and correctly.

1 2 3 4 5   (your own goal) _____

1 2 3 4 5   (your own goal) _____

If you've given yourself a 3 or lower on any of these goals:

- visit the *Tapestry* web site for additional practice.

- ask your instructor for extra help.

- review the sections of the chapter that you found difficult.

- work with a partner or study group to further your progress.

L ook closely at the photo, and then discuss these questions with your classmates:

- Do you see a story in this photo?

- Have you read any stories about families? What stories have you read on this subject?

- Do you enjoy reading about others' families? Why or why not?

8

ANALYZING: ALL IN THE FAMILY

Writing about and discussing literature are important parts of an education in English. This chapter will provide you with tools to discuss and analyze literature effectively. In order to analyze a story effectively, you typically have to do a *close* reading—reading it once for the overall ideas and plot, then rereading the story to focus on specific features of the writing itself.

Setting Goals

This chapter will provide you with some strategies and skills for analyzing and writing about literature. You will learn how to:

◈ write effective thesis statements for analytical writing.

◈ prepare for quizzes to help you in your classes.

◈ use specialized vocabulary to write about literature.

◈ make paragraphs coherent and unified.

What other goals do you have for learning about analytical writing? Write two more here:

_____

_____

⟨Getting Started

As you read a work of fiction, it is important to ask questions about the story:

- How does it make you feel?

- Why do the main characters behave the way they do?

- What changes take place during the story? Why are these changes important?

- What is the main problem of the story? How is the main problem resolved?

By thinking about these questions, as well as any others that occur to you, you will be able to solve some of the mysteries of understanding fiction.

With a partner, identify a story you have both read, or a movie you have both seen and remember well. Answer the questions above.

TUNING IN: "The Bush Family"

© CNN

Watch the CNN video about the Bush family. Discuss these questions with your class:

- Who are the Bushes?

- How many Bush relatives are mentioned in the story?

- What kinds of careers do they have?

- What kind of person is Barbara Bush?

- What kind of father is George Bush?

In your journal, respond to this question:

Would you like one of your relatives to become a world leader? Why or why not?

LANGUAGE LEARNING STRATEGY

Use specialized vocabulary to write about literature more precisely. It is not necessary to have a specialized vocabulary in order to discuss literature, but it is helpful. Just as doctors or engineers have special words for discussing their work, writers who analyze literature use specialized terminology. This makes discussing literature easier, because you can use precise vocabulary rather than long descriptions.

Here are some common literary terms and definitions:

1. **Plot** is the order of events in a story. Traditional plots are usually told in chronological order, that is, according to a time sequence. But **flashbacks,** or memories of scenes that came before the story, may also be used. The plot depends on some sort of **conflict,** and as it develops, this conflict usually develops into a **crisis,** a major event in the story in which the main character must take some action or make a decision. This decision leads to the story's **resolution,** or conclusion. The plots of short stories might seem less dramatic or conclusive than those of novels. Therefore, you may want to read shorter works more closely for a clearer understanding.

2. **Characters** are the people in a story. The description of the personality, appearance, and actions is called **development.** Characters are either "major" or "minor": major characters have complex personalities and undergo changes and crises; minor characters support the plot and actions of the main characters, but usually we learn less about them, and they usually don't change significantly.

    The main character is called the **protagonist,** and the person or force who acts against this character is called the **antagonist.** A protagonist isn't necessarily a "positive" or "good" character, just the main character; similarly, the antagonist isn't necessarily negative or evil.

3. When you read a story, a **narrator** tells the story from a particular **point of view.** (The author of the story typically is *not* the narrator.) Below are the most popular choices for point of view:

    - **First person:** In first-person point of view, the narrator uses the pronoun *I* and plays a part in the story. The first-person narrator can be a major or minor character. If a first-person point of view is used, then the narrator's involvement in the story affects the reporting of the events, and the potential bias of the narrator is an important part of the analysis.

    - **Third person:** Third-person point of view is told by a narrator who is not directly involved in the story. There are two kinds of third-person narrators: **omniscient** and **limited omniscient.** The omniscient narrator can see behind the thoughts and

(continued on next page)

motivations of all the characters and tell the story from every perspective. The limited-omniscient narrator can usually see into only the major characters' thoughts.

4. The **setting** is the time, place, and context in which a story takes place. The setting informs us of the history and environment in which the characters act. Elements of the setting, such as the seasons of the year, or natural phenomena, such as an ocean or a thunderstorm, may act as a force of action in the story, just as a character does.

5. A **symbol** is an object or an action that represents something else, typically, a more complicated or abstract idea. Symbols are important to a story because they increase its depth and complexity. It helps to understand symbols, but it is also important not to see everything as a potential symbol or to "read meaning into" things that may not be symbols.

6. **Style** refers to the language and construction of a story. For example, a writer might write in a dialect to show the regional origins of the characters. Or the writer may compose a highly symbolic and abstract story, or one that has a lot of action. Style has different elements, but two of the major elements are tone and irony:

   • **Tone** relates to the mood of the story. Think of tone as a story's "personality." Is it serious? Depressing? Tragic? Joyful? Optimistic? Some mixture of these? To understand tone, look at the word choice, the imagery, and the symbols that the author uses.

   • **Irony** occurs when the actions don't match the intentions of the characters, or don't match the reader's predictions. Individual words or phrases can also be used ironically, when a character says the opposite of what he or she really means.

7. The **theme** is a major idea in a story. It is sometimes difficult to define a theme, however, because there may be more than one. Also, different readers may interpret the theme differently—there's no one absolute, "correct" theme. That's why literature is analyzed—each reader may have a slightly different understanding of what is important and interesting in a work of fiction.

Apply the Strategy

As you read the first story, complete the following chart, identifying the story's important elements. Then compare and discuss your answers with your classmates. You may want to make several photocopies of this table, or use a separate piece of paper, because you will use this table for other stories as well.

	Description
Characters: Major: Protagonist: Antagonist: Minor:	
Setting:	
Point of view:	
Plot summary (brief):	
Style: Tone: Irony:	
Conflict:	
Theme:	
Symbolism:	

◆ **Getting Ready to Read**   You will first read the story "Crickets," by Robert Olen Butler. As you read it, take notes, identifying the elements in the definitions in the "Language Learning Strategy."

◆ **Vocabulary Check**   These words are in the reading. How many do you know? Check them. Discuss the words with a classmate, and explain any that you know that your partner does not. Then write a definition or an example sentence in your Vocabulary Log.

_____ agitation _____ corny _____ ploy

_____ bowler _____ cowling _____ refinery

_____ bullion

◆ **Read**   ## Reading 1: Crickets

by Robert Olen Butler

1   They call me Ted where I work and they've called me that for over a decade now and it still bothers me, though I'm not very happy about my real name being the same as the former President of the former Republic of Vietnam. Thiêu is not an uncommon name in my homeland and my mother had nothing more in mind than a long-dead uncle when she gave it to me. But in Lake Charles, Louisiana, I am Ted. I guess the other Mr. Thiêu has enough of my former country's former gold **bullion** tucked away so that in London, where he probably wears a **bowler** and carries a rolled umbrella, nobody's calling him anything but Mr. Thiêu.

2   I hear myself sometimes and I sound pretty bitter, I guess. But I don't let that out at the **refinery,** where I'm the best chemical engineer they've got and they even admit it once in a while. They're good-hearted people, really. I've done enough fighting in my life. I was eighteen when Saigon fell and I was only recently mustered into the Army, and when my unit dissolved and everybody ran, I stripped off my uniform and put on my civilian clothes again and I threw rocks at the North's tanks when they rolled through the streets. Very few of my people did likewise. I stayed in the mouths of alleys so I could run and then return and throw more rocks, but because what I did seemed so isolated and so pathetic a gesture, the gunners in the tanks didn't even take notice. But I didn't care about their scorn. At least my right arm had said no to them.

3   And then there were Thai Pirates in the South China Sea and idiots running the refugee centers and more idiots running the agencies in the U.S. to find a place for me and my new bride, who braved with me the midnight escape by boat and the terrible sea and all the rest. We ended up here in the flat bayou land of Louisiana, where there are rice paddies and where the water and the land are in the most delicate balance with each other, very much like the Mekong Delta, where I grew up. These people who work around me are good people and maybe they call me Ted because they want to think of me as one of them, though sometimes it bothers me that these men are so much bigger than me. I am the size of a woman in this country and these American men are all massive and they speak so slowly, even to one another, even though English is their native language. I've heard New Yorkers on television and I speak as fast as they do.

4   My son is beginning to speak like the others here in Louisiana. He is ten, the product of the

first night my wife and I spent in Lake Charles, in a cheap motel with the sky outside red from the refineries. He is proud to have been born in America, and when he leaves us in the morning to walk to the Catholic school, he says, "Have a good day, y'all." Sometimes I say good-bye to him in Vietnamese and he wrinkles his nose at me and says, "Aw, Pop," like I'd just cracked a **corny** joke. He doesn't speak Vietnamese at all and my wife says not to worry about that. He's an American.

5   But I do worry about that, though I understand why I should be content. I even understood ten years ago, so much so that I agreed with my wife and gave my son an American name. Bill. Bill and his father Ted. But this past summer I found my son hanging around the house bored in the middle of vacation and I was suddenly his father Thiêu with a wonderful idea for him. It was an idea that had come to me in the first week of every February we'd been in Lake Charles, because that's when the crickets always begin to crow here. This place is rich in crickets, which always make me think of my own childhood in Vietnam. But I never said anything to my son until last summer.

6   I came to him after watching him slouch around the yard one Sunday pulling the Spanish moss off the lowest branches of our big oak tree and then throwing rocks against the stop sign on our corner. "Do you want to do something fun?" I said to him.

7   "Sure, Pop," he said, though there was a certain suspicion in his voice, like he didn't trust me on the subject of fun. He threw all the rocks at once that were left in his hand and the stop sign shivered at their impact.

8   I said, "If you keep that up, they will arrest me for the destruction of city property and then they will deport us all."

9   My son laughed at this. I, of course, knew that he would know I was bluffing. I didn't want to be too hard on him for the boyish impulses that I myself had found to be so satisfying when I was young, especially since I was about to share something of my own childhood with him.

10   "So what've you got, Pop?" my son asked me.

11   "Fighting crickets," I said.

12   "What?"

13   Now, my son was like any of his fellow ten-year-olds, devoted to superheroes and the mighty clash of good and evil in all of its high-tech forms in the Saturday-morning cartoons. Just to make sure he was in the right frame of mind, I explained it to him with one word, "Cricketmen," and I thought this was a pretty good **ploy.** He cocked his head in interest at this and I took him to the side porch and sat him down and I explained.

14   I told him how, when I was a boy, my friends and I would prowl the undergrowth and capture crickets and keep them in matchboxes. We would feed them leaves and bits of watermelon and bean sprouts, and we'd train them to fight by keeping them in a constant state of **agitation** by blowing on them and gently flicking the ends of their antennas with a sliver of wood. So each of us would have a stable of fighting crickets, and there were two kinds.

15   At this point my son was squirming a little bit and his eyes were shifting away into the yard and I knew that my Cricketman trick had run its course. I fought back the urge to challenge his set of interests. Why should the stiff and foolish fights of his cartoon characters absorb him and the real clash—real life and death—that went on in the natural world bore him? But I realized that I hadn't cut to the chase yet, as they say on the TV. "They fight to the death," I said with as much gravity as I could put into my voice, like I was James Earl Jones.

16   The announcement won me a glance and a brief lift of his eyebrows. This gave me a little scrabble of panic, because I still hadn't told him about the two types of crickets and I suddenly knew that was a real important part for me. I tried not to despair at his understanding and I put my hands on his shoulders and turned him around to face me. "Listen," I sad. "You need to understand this if you are to

have fighting crickets. There are two types, and all of us had some of each. One type we called the charcoal crickets. These were very large and strong, but they were slow and they could become confused. The other type was small and brown and we called them fire crickets. They weren't as strong, but they were very smart and quick."

17   "So who would win?" my son said.

18   "Sometimes one and sometimes the other. The fights were very long and full of hard struggle. We'd have a little tunnel made of paper and we'd slip a sliver of wood under the **cowling** of our cricket's head to make him mad and we'd twirl him by his antenna, and then we'd each put our cricket into the tunnel at opposite ends. Inside, they'd approach each other and begin to fight and then we'd lift the paper tunnel and watch."

19   "Sounds neat," my son said, though his enthusiasm was at best moderate, and I knew I had to act quickly.

20   So we got a shoe box and we started looking for crickets. It's better at night, but I knew for sure his interest wouldn't last that long. Our house is up on blocks because of the high water table in town and we crawled along the edge, pulling back the bigger tufts of grass and turning over rocks. It was one of the rocks that gave us our first crickets, and my son saw them and cried in my ear, "There, there," but he waited for me to grab them. I cupped first one and then the other and dropped them into the shoe box and I felt a vague disappointment, not so much because it was clear that my boy did not want to touch the insects, but that they were both the big black ones, the charcoal crickets. We crawled on and we found another one in the grass and another sitting in the muddy shadow of the house behind the hose faucet and then we caught two more under an azalea bush.

21   "Isn't that enough?" my son demanded. "How many do we need?"

22   I sat with my back against the house and put the shoe box in my lap and my boy sat be-side me, his head stretching this way so he could look into the box. There was no more vagueness to my feeling. I was actually weak with disappointment because all six of these were charcoal crickets, big and inert and just looking around like they didn't even know anything was wrong.

23   "Oh, no," my son said with real force, and for a second I thought he had read my mind and shared my feeling, but I looked at him and he was pointing at the toes of his white sneakers. "My Reeboks are ruined!" he cried, and on the toe of each sneaker was a smudge of grass.

24   I glanced back into the box and the crickets had not moved and I looked at my son and he was still staring at his sneakers. "Listen," I said, "this was a big mistake. You can go on and do something else."

25   He jumped up at once. "Do you think Mom can clean these?" he said.

26   "Sure," I said. "Sure."

27   He was gone at once and the side door slammed and I put the box on the grass. But I didn't go in. I got back on my hands and knees and I circled the entire house and then I turned over every stone in the yard and dug around all the trees. I found probably two dozen more crickets, but they were all the same. In Louisiana there are rice paddies and some of the bayous look like the Delta, but many of the birds are different, and why shouldn't the insects be different, too? This is another country, after all. It was just funny about the fire crickets. All of us kids rooted for them, even if we were fighting with one of our own charcoal crickets. A fire cricket was a very precious and admirable thing.

28   The next morning my son stood before me as I finished my breakfast and once he had my attention, he looked down at his feet, drawing my eyes down as well. "See?" he said. "Mom got them clean."

29   Then he was out the door and I called after him, "See you later, Bill."

After You Read

About the Content

1. What is the primary conflict in this story? Are there others? How are the conflicts resolved?

2. What do you think the crickets symbolize? Why does Butler distinguish between charcoal crickets and fire crickets?

3. Identify an important theme in this story. What other themes can you identify?

4. What is your reaction to this story? With whom do you sympathize?

5. How does Ted change?

The family is one of nature's masterpieces.

—GEORGE SANTAYANA

About the Writing

1. Identify at least one example where the author uses irony.

2. Describe the tone of "Crickets." What words or phrases illustrate this tone?

3. What is the significance of the last paragraph of this story? Is it an effective way to end?

Quickwrite

Write for 10 minutes on this subject: Can you recall a time when you had a conflict in philosophy with a family member? Describe what happened.

Getting Ready to Read

The next story also deals with family drama. As you read it, again take notes, identifying the elements in the definitions from pages 140–143.

Vocabulary Check

These words and phrases are in the reading. How many do you know? Check them. Discuss the words with a classmate, and explain any that you know that your partner does not. Then write a definition or an example sentence in your Vocabulary Log.

_____ barbarian   _____ mourners

_____ disposition   _____ rosary

_____ fiendish   _____ sown

_____ full-steam ahead   _____ spitting image

Read

Reading 2: Grandma's Wake

by Emilio Díaz Valcárcel

1   We welcomed Uncle Segundo this morning. We sat waiting on one of the benches at the airport for four hours while mobs of people came and went. The people were looking at us and saying things and I was thinking how it would be to ride in an airplane and leave behind the *barrio*[1], my friends in school, Mamá moaning about the bad times and the cafés that don't let anybody sleep. And then to live talking other words, far from the river where we bathe every afternoon. That's what I was thinking about this morning, dead tired because we'd gotten up at five. A few planes arrived but Uncle Segundo wasn't to be seen anywhere. Mamá was saying that he hadn't changed a bit, that he was the same old Segundo, arriving late at places, and probably mixed up with the police. That he'd probably got in some kind of a jam up there in the North and they'd arrested him, that he hadn't paid the store and was in court. That's what Mamá was saying, looking all around her, asking people, cursing every time they stepped on her new slippers.

2   I'd never met Uncle Segundo. They said that he had my face and that if I had a mustache we'd be like made to order. That's what the big people argued about on Sunday afternoon when Aunt Altagracia came from San Juan with her bag full of smells and sweets, and told us to ask her for a blessing and then talked with Mamá about how drawn and skinny I was, and whether I attended Sunday school and whether I studied, after which they would almost come to blows because Aunt Altagracia would say that I was Segundo through and through. Mamá didn't like it at first, but later she would say yes, that I was really another Segundo in the flesh, except without the mustache. But one thing, my aunt would snap, let's hope he doesn't have his **fiendish** nature, for one time someone called him "one ear" and he slashed the man's back and he also castrated the dog that ripped up the pants he wore for calling on his women. And Mamá would say no, I wouldn't have her brother's high-flown **disposition**, 'cause I was more like a sick little mouse if you were to judge by the way I sneaked around. Then Mamá would send me for a nickel's worth of cigarettes or to milk the goat, so that I wouldn't hear when she began to talk of Papá, and of the nights she couldn't sleep waiting for him while he played dominoes in Eufrasio's, and my aunt would turn all red and say she had it coming to her and that they'd warned her plenty and told her don't be crazy that man's a barfly don't be crazy watch what you're doing.

3   That was every Sunday, the only day that Aunt Altagracia could come from San Juan and visit this *barrio,* which she says she hates because the people don't have manners. But today is Tuesday and she came to see Grandma and to wait for her brother, because they wrote him that Grandma was on her last legs and he said all right if that's the way it is I'm coming but I've go to leave right away. And we were waiting four hours at the airport, dead tired, while all the people looked at us and said things.

4   Neither Mamá nor Aunt Altagracia recognized the man who came up dressed in white, looking plenty smooth and fat. He threw himself into their arms and nearly squeezed them both dry at the same time. As for me, he gave a tug at my sideburns and then stared at me awhile, then he picked me up and told me I was a real he-man and asked if I had a girlfriend.

[1] *barrio:* Spanish for "neighborhood."

Mamá said that I'd been born a bit sickly and that from what I'd **sown** so far I'd turn out to be a sick little mouse. Aunt Altagracia said that they should take a good look, a real good look, for if I had a mustache I'd be the double in miniature of my uncle.

5   During the trip Uncle Segundo talked about his business in the North. My mother and my aunt both agreed that someday they would go up there, because here the sun makes one age ahead of time, and the work, the heat, the few opportunities to improve one's life. . . . We reached home without my being aware of it. Uncle Segundo woke me up tugging hard at my ear and asking if I could see God and saying straighten up 'cause nobody pays attention to people who hang their heads.

6   Uncle Segundo found Grandma a bit pale, but not as bad as they'd told him. He put his hand on her chest and told her to breathe, to come on and breathe, and he nearly turned the bed over and threw Grandma on the floor. He patted her on the face and then claimed she was all right, and that he'd come from so far away and that he'd left his business all alone and this was the only—listen, you— the *only* chance right now. Because after all he'd come to a funeral, and nothing else. My mother and my aunt opened their mouths to yell and they said it was true, he hadn't changed a bit. But my uncle said the old woman was fine, look at her, and what would people say if he couldn't come back from the North for the funeral next time? And he said it plenty clear: it had to happen in the three days he was going to spend in the *barrio* and if not they'd have to give him back the money he'd spent on the trip. My mamá and my aunt had their hands to their heads yelling **barbarian,** you're nothing but a heretic barbarian. Uncle Segundo's neck swelled up, he started saying things I didn't understand and he took

Grandma's measurements. He measured her with his hands from head to foot and side to side. Grandma was smiling and it looked like she wanted to talk to him. Uncle made a face and went looking for Santo, the carpenter, and told him to make a coffin of the best wood there was, that his family wasn't cheap. They spoke about the price for a while and then Uncle left to see the four women he's got in the *barrio.* He gave each one six bits[2] and brought them over to our house. They lit a few candles and put Grandma in the coffin where she could've danced, she was so skinny. My uncle complained and said the coffin was too wide, that Santo had made it like that just to charge more, and that he wouldn't pay a cent over three fifty. Grandma kept on laughing there, inside the coffin, and moved her lips like she wanted to say something. Uncle's women hadn't begun to cry when two of their dogs started to fight beneath the coffin. Uncle Segundo was furious and he kicked them until they peed and came out from under and left, their tails between their legs, yelping. Then Uncle moved his hand up and down and the women began to cry and shout. Uncle pinched them so they'd make more noise. Mamá was stretched out on the floor, howling just like the dogs; Aunt Altagracia was fanning her and sprinkling her with *alcoholado.* Papá was there, lying down at her side, saying that these things do happen and that it was all their fault, 'cause if they hadn't said anything to his brother-in-law nothing would have happened.

7   All that yelling began to draw people to the wake. Papá wasn't too happy about Eufrasio coming because he was always trying to collect debts with those hard looks of his. The twins, Serafin and Evaristo, arrived, and they tossed a coin heads or tails to see who would lead the **rosary.** Chalí came up with his eight children and sat them down on the floor and

[2]**six bits:** an old-fashioned way of saying 75 cents. Two bits is a quarter, or 25 cents.

searched them for bugs while he mumbled his prayers. The Cané sisters came in through the kitchen looking at the cupboard, fanning themselves with a newspaper and saying things in each other's ears. The dogs were fighting outside. Cañón came up to Mamá and said he congratulated her, 'cause these things, well, they have to happen and that God Almighty would fix things up so as to find a little corner on his throne for the poor old woman. Aunt Altagracia was saying that the wake would have been more proper in San Juan and not in this damned *barrio*, which she unfortunately had to visit. Uncle Segundo was telling Grandma to shut her damned mouth, not to laugh, for this was no joke but a wake where she, though it mightn't not seem so, was the most important thing.

8   Mamá got up and took Grandma out of the coffin. She was carrying her toward the room when Uncle, drunk and saying bad words, grabbed Grandma by the head and began to pull her back toward the coffin. Mamá kept pulling her by the ankles and then the dogs came in and started to bark. Uncle Segundo threw them a kick. The dogs left, but my uncle went sideways and fell on the floor with Mamá and Grandma. Papá squatted down next to Mamá and told her that this was incredible, that they should please their brother after all the years he'd been away. But Mamá didn't give in and then Uncle began to stamp his feet and Aunt Altagracia said, see, this boy hasn't changed a bit.

9   But my uncle still got things his way. Cañón was stretching out in a corner crying. The Cané sisters came up to my grandma and said how pretty the old woman looks, still smiling as in life, how pretty, eh?

10   I felt sort of shrunk. My uncle was a big strong man. I, Mamá herself said it, will turn out to be just a sick little mouse, the way I'm going. I would like to be strong, like my uncle, and fight anyone who gets in my way. I felt tiny whenever my uncle looked at me and said that

I wouldn't look like him even with a mustache, that they'd fooled him so many times, and what was this? He would end up telling me that I'd become the **spitting image** of my father, and that one couldn't expect much from someone with my looks.

11   Cañón began to talk with Rosita Cané and after a while they went into the kitchen, acting as if they weren't up to something. The other Cané was fanning herself with a paper and looking enviously toward the kitchen and also looking at Eufrasio who, they say, bought off Melina's parents with a refrigerator. Melina had left to give birth someplace else and since then Eufrasio just drinks and fights with customers. But now Eufrasio was nice and calm and he was looking at the Cané girl and talking sign-language. He came up with a bottle and offered her a drink and she said heavens how dare you, but then she hid behind the curtain and if Eufrasio hadn't taken the bottle away she wouldn't have left a drop.

12   The wake was now going **full-steam ahead** and the twins kept leading the rosary, looking toward the room where Aunt Altagracia was lying down. I was nearly asleep when the beating Uncle Segundo gave Cañón shook me up. My uncle was shouting and demanding to know what kind of things were going on and that they should all leave if each and every one of them didn't want to get their share. Rosita Cané was crying. My uncle grabbed his suitcase and said that all in all he was satisfied because he'd come to his mother's wake and that now he didn't have to go through it again. He went out saying that he didn't mind paying for the fare, or the box, or the **mourners**, and that in the whole *barrio* they wouldn't find such a sacrificing son. There's the coffin, he said, for whoever's turn it is. And he left, almost running.

13   When I went up to the coffin and looked at Grandma she wasn't laughing anymore. But I noticed a tiny bit of brightness flowing from her eyes and wetting her tightly closed lips.

ACADEMIC POWER STRATEGY

Prepare for quizzes to help you in your classes. Most instructors give quizzes to their students to check how well they are understanding the material studied in class. Quizzes provide a good way to be sure that students are keeping up and understanding the work. Occasionally, you might even have a quiz that the instructor doesn't announce; these are called "pop quizzes."

Here are some ways to prepare for a quiz:

1. Always keep up with your work the best you can. If you've done the reading and homework, chances are you'll be prepared, even for pop quizzes.

2. Take good notes. Use whatever note-taking system works best for you. Taking notes helps you synthesize and understand your class material.

3. Review with a study group. Talking through the material with classmates can help you clarify areas you didn't fully understand.

Apply the Strategy

Quiz

Answer the following questions without consulting the first part of this chapter. You may look back at the story, however.

1. Name and describe the *protagonist* of the story.

2. Name and describe the *antagonist* of the story.

3. Who are the *minor characters*? Describe each of them.

4. Briefly describe the *setting* of this story.

5. Who is the *narrator*, and what *point of view* is the story written from?

6. What is the major *conflict*?

7. Identify one *symbol*.

8. Identify one major element of *style* in the story.

9. What do you think the *theme* of this story is?

10. Briefly summarize the *plot*.

After You Read

About the Content

1. Why are people at the airport "saying things" about the narrator and his family?

2. What kind of person is Uncle Segundo? What physical characteristics does he have that emphasize his personality traits?

3. What are the people of the *barrio* like?

4. What is the typical meaning of "holding a wake"? In what way is this a different sort of wake?

5. Why did Papá feel it important to please their brother Segundo?

6. What is the symbolism of "the North" in this story?

About the Writing

1. Whose point of view is this story told from? Why did the author choose this character, in your opinion? How would a different point of view change the story?

2. How is speech reported? Why did the author choose this method rather than direct dialogue, in your opinion?

3. Why did the author choose to use some Spanish words in this story? What effect does it have?

Quickwrite

Write about this topic for 15 minutes: Imagine you are the grandmother in this story. Write your feelings about what has taken place.

> All happy families are alike, but an unhappy family is unhappy after its own fashion.
>
> —*ANNA KARENINA,*
> BY LEO TOLSTOY

FROM READING TO WRITING

You have read two stories about families, and learned the specialized vocabulary for talking about literature. Now you will use this terminology and the ways you have learned to think and talk about literature to write an analytical essay.

Getting Ready to Write

For this essay, you will develop your own writing topic. The subject for the paper is *the role of traditions in family life*. Write an essay on this subject using the two stories found in this chapter as well as your own experience and/or observations.

Write a strong thesis statement to make your writing clear. The assignment on the previous page gives you the subject matter for the essay. You need to decide on how you will narrow that subject area to a workable topic, and then a thesis statement. A good way to visualize this distinction is by imagining a triangle:

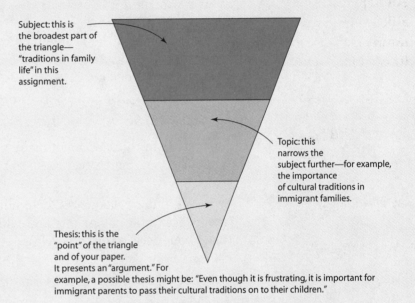

Subject: this is the broadest part of the triangle—"traditions in family life" in this assignment.

Topic: this narrows the subject further—for example, the importance of cultural traditions in immigrant families.

Thesis: this is the "point" of the triangle and of your paper. It presents an "argument." For example, a possible thesis might be: "Even though it is frustrating, it is important for immigrant parents to pass their cultural traditions on to their children."

For most types of college or expository writing, the success of your essay depends on a strong thesis statement. A thesis presents a specific argument or point you want to make.

Thesis statements are composed of two major elements: a **topic** and a **comment**. The topic is the part of the thesis that states generally what subject matter is discussed, and the comment specifies one important point relating to the topic. For example:

In the stories "Crickets" and "Grandma's Wake,"

topic

the theme of xxx plays an important role.

comment

(continued on next page)

The thesis statement represents the writer's interpretation of a topic—for that reason, it should make an interesting and arguable claim. In order to be arguable, it must try to convince the audience of something that the audience may disagree with, or may not have considered previously. Therefore, the following sentence is not a thesis statement:

> *"Crickets" tells the story of a Vietnamese immigrant and his American-born son.*

This statement is an **observation**—that is, it states a fact with which no one could disagree.

In addition, a thesis statement needs to focus on one idea and not try to argue for several issues at once. The following example tries to do too much:

> *Reading literature provides an important way of understanding a culture; furthermore, it is a relaxing hobby.*

Both parts of this statement make a point—but they are two separate ideas and, therefore, belong to two separate essays.

Apply the Strategy

With a group of classmates, determine which of the following statements are thesis statements and which are not. Be prepared to explain your decisions to your class.

1. The main characters of "Grandma's Wake" and "Crickets" are poor.

2. In order to be a good writer, you must also read a lot of literature.

3. Many writers record their ideas in journals.

4. Some people enjoy literature while others do not; it's a matter of taste.

5. Even though the main characters of "Grandma's Wake" and "Crickets" are very different, their problems are similar.

6. It is important to build a book collection of works you enjoy; in addition, you should read magazines often.

7. The plot of "Crickets" involves a young boy, Bill, and a game his father wants to play with crickets.

Now write a *draft thesis statement* (it doesn't have to be a perfect, final thesis statement). Put your thesis statement on the chalkboard in your classroom for analysis by your classmates. When looking at your own and your classmates' thesis statements, discuss the following questions for each:

- Is the thesis statement arguable?
- Is it a single sentence?
- Is it interesting?
- Is there enough information to support it?
- Is it grammatical?
- Is it specific (that is, does it make only one point)?

After your discussion, make any changes to your thesis statement that you think are necessary.

Write

When you have formulated a good thesis, assemble the materials you will need to begin your draft. These include:

- Notes from your reading and class discussion
- Relevant quickwrite topics
- Notes on personal experience that you want to include
- Quotations from your reading that support your thesis

If you don't have enough information to get started, review your reading and find quotations, freewrite on your thesis, and review your notes and memories of class discussions. Once you have your materials assembled, begin by writing an outline of your paper. An outline can be in any form you are familiar or comfortable with—it can be a list, a formal outline (with Roman numerals and letters), or any other format that works for you.

You are now ready to write your first draft.

After You Write

Revise

After you have completed your draft, fill out the following information and include it with a copy of your essay. Bring your paper and this top sheet to class and exchange them with a classmate. Read your partner's paper, answer his or her questions, and respond with any ideas you have.

Draft Top Sheet
1. Please tell me . . .
2. The part of my paper I am most concerned about is . . .
3. Other questions I have are . . .

Feature	Problem	Possible Solution
Title		
Opening paragraph		
Examples		
Organization		
Word choice		
Conclusion		
Other		

Remember that revision is not merely correcting your spelling and grammar, and inserting a few commas. In the revision phase of the writing process, you are reorganizing, cutting, adding detail, and improving your choices. Looking at the review you received from your partner and your response to it, formulate a revision plan. Use the chart on the previous page to help you identify the areas that need the most improvement.

Use your revision plan to guide your rewriting.

Grammar You Can Use: Paragraph Unity and Coherence

If you look at different types of writing, you will notice that paragraph lengths and structures vary a great deal. However, in expository writing, each paragraph typically requires the following elements:

- A **topic sentence** that reports the main idea
- **Development** of the main idea through examples
- **Coherence** of word choice and of sequence of ideas

The **topic sentence** states what the paragraph is about. All the sentences in the paragraph should relate to this idea—this is called **unity.** Your topic sentence can be placed anywhere in your paragraph.

In your draft, underline the topic sentence in each paragraph. Then reread the paragraph sentence by sentence. Does each sentence relate to your topic? If not, put an x by it, and consider eliminating or moving it.

In addition to your main idea, each paragraph needs **development** of that idea—that is, examples or other information that explains your main idea. Reread each paragraph in your draft and make a note in the margin showing what kind of development you use:

- Example from your own experience
- Definition of a word
- Example or quotation from reading
- Explanation of an event
- Personal opinion
- Other (label it with a name)

Now look at your margin notes. How balanced is your development? Do you have a variety of types of support, or do you tend to use only your own opinion? If necessary, make notes about what changes you need to balance your examples.

Coherence in a paragraph (and in an essay) means that the word choices and sequence of ideas fit together in a logical way and draw attention to the most important concepts. Coherence can be achieved in many ways. Three major techniques are using transitions, repeating key words and ideas, and using parallel structures. Look at the following passage:

> Macaws nest in cozy tree cavities a hundred feet or more off the ground. Two questions loomed as I set out to investigate macaw reproduction. *How would I get up there*, and *how would the birds react once I did*?
>
> I **start** with a giant slingshot, launching a weight on a thin line over *a branch* near the nest. **Then** I tie *a climbing rope* to the unweighted end and pull the weighted end by hand **until** *the rope* is hanging over *the branch*.
>
> —by Charles A. Munn

In the first paragraph, the single underlined phrases refer to the same things, the macaws. The double-underlined phrases refer to the position of the climber ("up there"). The italicized last sentence shows a parallel structure—two questions formed in the same way, making up part of a complex sentence.

The second paragraph shows the author's use of transitions, shown in boldface, as well as more use of repeated phrases to obtain coherence. These techniques help the reader keep track of the order of the story and the main ideas.

Finally, examine your own writing again. In each of your paragraphs, identify your transitions, the repetition of key words and phrases, and parallel structures; then ask yourself the following questions:

- **Transitions:** Do you supply enough guidance for your reader? Is the sequence of events or ideas made clearer through your use of transitions?

- **Keywords:** Do you highlight the main ideas in your writing by repeating keywords and concepts? Do you repeat the same word *too* frequently? If so, use synonyms or rewrite in a way to avoid unnecessary repetition.

- **Parallel Structures:** Is each part of a parallel structure in the same grammatical form as the other? For example,

    Parallel: I enjoy *reading, cooking, and watching TV.*

    Not Parallel: I like *swimming, fishing, and to hike.*

> If I were to prescribe one process in the training of men which is fundamental to success in any direction, it would be thoroughgoing training in the habit of accurate observation. It is a habit which every one of us should be seeking ever more to perfect.
>
> **—EUGENE G. GRACE**

Self-Correction

In your essay assignment, identify areas where you had difficulty with paragraphs. Rewrite any paragraphs with errors in them.

Edit

After you have solved the problems identified in your revision plan, you can focus on editing and proofreading your paper. The editing phase includes double-checking your grammar, spelling, punctuation, and so forth. Each student has unique problems in this area, so it may be helpful to take an inventory of problem spots, based on your past experience as a writer. Remember, you can change this inventory as you progress.

Which of the following items do you think are a problem for you? Check the appropriate column.

PROBLEM	MAJOR PROBLEM	MINOR PROBLEM	NO PROBLEM	DON'T KNOW
Spelling	_____	_____	_____	_____
Punctuation	_____	_____	_____	_____
Subject–verb agreement	_____	_____	_____	_____
Verb tenses	_____	_____	_____	_____
Articles	_____	_____	_____	_____
Prepositions	_____	_____	_____	_____
Plurals	_____	_____	_____	_____
Sentence fragments	_____	_____	_____	_____
Run-on sentences	_____	_____	_____	_____
Wordiness	_____	_____	_____	_____
Parallel structures	_____	_____	_____	_____

If you have checked more than three as a "major problem," decide which three you would like to work on first. It's easier to concentrate on a few problem areas at a time.

The last step should be proofreading—that is, looking for careless mistakes: misspellings, leaving out words, typing words twice in a row, and so forth. Before you turn your paper in, proofread it carefully.

PUTTING IT ALL TOGETHER

◇ **A Personal Anthology**

An **anthology** is a collection of writings put together into one collection. Anthologies can have themes, such as short stories about families, or they can be more general, such as a collection of essays on different topics.

For this activity, you and a group of classmates will create your own anthology. Here are the steps for doing so:

1. Visit your library to locate sources of short stories that interest you. You can find short stories in books or in magazines.

2. With a small group of classmates, identify five stories that you enjoy and would recommend to your classmates.

3. Write a short review and introduction to each story.

4. Include information about the authors, and other notes of interest.

5. Make a photocopy of each of the stories and put them into the folder, along with your review material.

6. Share your anthology with your classmates.

Test-Taking Tip

Learn special techniques for multiple-choice tests. Multiple-choice tests have the reputation for being easier than those with essay questions. However, don't be fooled. Multiple choice tests can be difficult. Here are a few techniques to apply to these kinds of tests:

- Answer a question in your head before you choose one of the options.

- Read all the choices before selecting one.

- If two answers are similar except for one or two words, choose one of those two.

- If you need to complete a sentence, eliminate answers that aren't grammatical.

- If you are uncertain and there is no penalty for guessing, choose any answer!

CHECK YOUR PROGRESS

On a scale of 1 to 5, rate how well you have mastered the goals set at the beginning of the chapter:

1 2 3 4 5   write effective thesis statements for analytical writing.

1 2 3 4 5   prepare for quizzes to help you in your classes.

1 2 3 4 5   use specialized vocabulary to write about literature.

1 2 3 4 5   make paragraphs coherent and unified.

1 2 3 4 5   (your own goal) _____

1 2 3 4 5   (your own goal) _____

If you've given yourself a 3 or lower on any of these goals:

- visit the *Tapestry* web site for additional practice.

- ask your instructor for extra help.

- review the sections of the chapter that you found difficult.

- work with a partner or study group to further your progress.

L ook closely at the photos, and then discuss these questions with your classmates:

• Do you enjoy reading letters to the editor of your newspaper?

• Have you ever written one yourself?

• Do you enjoy political debates? Why or why not?

9

PERSUADING: MAKING A CASE

Almost every type of writing involves an element of persuasion—trying to convince your reader to agree with you. However, there are certain types of writing particularly associated with persuasion: editorials and letters to the editor, advertising and letters of appeal, and essays arguing for political, religious, or economic causes. In this chapter, we will discover some of the elements of persuasion, and what makes for effective persuasive writing.

Setting Goals

This chapter will provide you with some strategies and techniques for writing effective arguments. In this chapter, you will learn how to:

◈ examine writing for important features you have learned.

◈ understand common problems/pitfalls in persuasive writing.

◈ work effectively in a group.

◈ eliminate wordiness in your writing.

What other goals do you have for learning to write persuasively? Write two more here.

_____

_____

Getting Started

As you read an argument, it is important to analyze it critically. Bring in a copy of a local or school newspaper, and look at the letters to the editor or an editorial essay. Read the letter or essay, and discuss these questions with a partner:

- What is the writer's argument?

- How does the writer support his or her argument?

- What kind of language does the writer use to convince you?

- Is the argument logical?

- What does the writer want you to do after understanding the argument?

> **The pen is the tongue of the mind.**
>
> **—MIGUEL DE CERVANTES**

By thinking about these questions, as well as any others that occur to you, you will be able to think clearly and critically about arguments, and not be persuaded by faulty logic.

Writing Tip: Elements of Persuasion

Many different methods can be used to persuade an audience. Here are some of the more common ones:

- **Appeal to Values:** Persuasive writing often appeals to an audience's sense of justice, fairness, and attitudes towards the community or world. Imagine that a large corporation is accused of polluting the environment. The company's marketing department might design a television commercial showing how the company has contributed to better ecological conditions. In this way, the writers try to appeal to the audience's belief in the value of protecting the environment.

- **Dramatize the Issue:** Good persuasive writing gets the audience's attention quickly and makes the audience react. If you are writing a fund-raising brochure for a homeless family shelter, you could start by listing the statistics on homelessness in your community. But, unfortunately, the facts alone may not attract your reader's attention. Instead, a more effective opening paragraph might tell the story of one homeless family. This would dramatically illustrate the problem and draw the reader into your argument.

- **Establish Authority:** The effectiveness of an argument often depends on the background of the writer. For example, if you are a nuclear physicist, you may be able to convince your readers of the dangers of nuclear power. If you are a local merchant who is worried about a new power plant in the community, you will have to take extra measures to convince your audience. Since a merchant probably doesn't have the expertise or any experience in nuclear physics, he or she needs to show the readers that he or she is knowledgeable. To do this, the merchant can quote experts and/or show that he or she has read widely about the subject by referring to information gotten from books and articles.

- **Use Effective Language:** The most effective persuasion uses words that are neither too strong nor too weak to explain the situation. If you are trying to convince your readers not to support a certain political candidate, you will probably use strong language that warns of the consequences of voting for that candidate. On the other hand, if you are advertising a new toy, you probably won't try to convince your readers that their lives will be ruined if they don't buy the toy for their children.

LANGUAGE LEARNING STRATEGY

Apply the Strategy

Examine writing for important features you have learned. So far in this book, you have learned to look at writing in two ways: first, for information, and second, for the features of the writing itself. When you look for features of writing, it helps you to remember the importance of these features, and it makes you a smarter reader *and* writer.

Bring a recent copy of a local or school newspaper to class. Read the editorials and letters to the editor. Underline or highlight uses of effective persuasion. Can you identify places where the writer could have been more persuasive? Discuss your findings with your classmates.

LANGUAGE LEARNING STRATEGY

Understand common problems/pitfalls in persuasive writing. Failing to capture your audience's attention and sympathy makes for weak persuasive writing. You can also make your argument ineffective by going too far—that is, by overstepping the bounds of logic and appropriateness. The following table presents some of the fallacies and weaknesses of persuasive writing—techniques that may make your audience feel unfairly manipulated, and thus react negatively to your argument.

FALLACY OR WEAKNESS	EXAMPLE
Ad hominem arguments Arguing against a person instead of against his or her beliefs or actions	"My opponent is not a college graduate; thus, he should not be allowed to speak publicly."
Bandwagon appeals Claiming that "everyone" believes a certain idea or does a certain thing; therefore, the reader is not "part of the crowd" if he or she believes otherwise	"All good patriots fly their flags on Independence Day; you don't want to be unpatriotic, do you?"
Exaggerated claims Overstating the causes or effects of an event or situation	"If we don't stop the excessive bridge tolls, our entire economy will collapse."
False analogies Comparing two things that aren't similar enough to compare	"People in cars don't have to wear helmets, so why should motorcycle riders?"
Misrepresentation Purposely leaving out facts in order to slant an argument	"Excessive television watching is no longer a major problem. Recent statistics show that network audiences have shrunk 54%." (This leaves out the fact that cable television audiences have grown 175%.)
Oversimplification Reducing complex problems into simple ones, or offering simplistic solutions to complicated problems	"The drug problem can be solved if we build more prisons."
Either-or thinking Arguing falsely that there are only two possible outcomes to a situation	"Either we require immigrants to learn English, or people won't be able to understand each other any longer."

Post hoc (ergo propter hoc)[1] *relationships*

Arguing that because an event happened before another one, it caused that event to happen.	"Ever since Ms. Blum was elected, unemployment has increased 5%." (In fact, perhaps the closing of a major factory contributed to the rise.)

Apply the Strategy   Read several letters to the editor of your school or local paper. Highlight places where you think there are logical fallacies. Bring in the newspaper and discuss these fallacies with your class.

TUNING IN: "Bilingual Education Controversy"

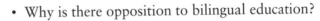

Watch the CNN video about bilingual education controversy. Discuss these questions with your class:

© CNN

- Why is there opposition to bilingual education?
- Why are some people in favor of bilingual education?
- Why are some parents opposed to it?
- Which side presented its case more convincingly in the story?
- Were there any weaknesses in the arguments you heard?

In your journal, respond to this question:

- What were your first experiences learning English like?

◇ Getting Ready to Read

> **Examine what is said, not who speaks.**
>
> —ARABIC PROVERB

Whether you work for a corporation and need to persuade customers to buy your products, or you work for a nonprofit organization and need to convince the public to contribute money to your organization, you need to use persuasion effectively. (Your job may depend on it!)

Every day, millions of pieces of mail are sent, asking for donations of money for worthwhile organizations. Read the following promotional material sent by Project Open Hand, a nonprofit organization in California.

[1]This phrase is Latin for "after the fact, therefore because of the fact."

◇Vocabulary Check

The words in this list are included in the reading. How many of them do you know? Check them. Look up the ones you don't, or discuss them with a classmate. Then, write a definition or example sentence in your Vocabulary Log.

_____ devastating   _____ malnutrition

_____ drastic   _____ replenish

◇Read   **Reading 1: Project Open Hand Kitchen**

THIS WEEK'S SHOPPING LIST

1,750 lbs	CHICKEN
1,500 lbs	BEEF
1,500 lbs	other meats such as TURKEY
$4,000	FRESH VEGETABLES, FRUITS & HERBS
360 lbs	BEANS
250 lbs	RICE
400 lbs	PASTA
150 ½	GALLONS OF MILK
400 lbs	HARD CHEESES AND TOFU
200	DOZEN EGGS
$8,000	VARIOUS GROCERIES

Clients can request regular meals, vegetarian meals or culturally specific.

Dear Friend,

Hello. I'm Martin Yan of Public Television's "Yan Can Cook" on KQED.

I've been actively involved with Project Open Hand for several years now. In fact, on a recent show I featured a recipe for "Rainbow chicken salad with glazed pecans" that's included in *The Open Hand Celebration Cookbook.*

But I'm not here to talk about myself. I'm going to talk about something more important: Food.

Ever since Ruth Brinker started Open Hand in 1985 by delivering meals she cooked herself to seven people with AIDS, Open Hand's mission has been to prepare meals using the freshest vegetables, fruit and meat.

Back then, no one could have foreseen how devastating the AIDS epidemic would become, or how many other people with AIDS would join those first seven clients in their need for home-delivered meals.

Today, over 10,000 people have died of AIDS in San Francisco alone. Currently, 28,000 are estimated to be infected with AIDS and HIV. Yet, despite these devastating statistics, Project Open has never had to turn down a request for help from a person with AIDS. That, I think you will agree, is nothing short of miraculous. And it's because of the caring and commitment of people from all over the Bay Area and beyond.

I'm asking you to join many of these wonderful, caring people.

As you can imagine, coming up with enough food is a daily battle. In fact, it's the single biggest challenge facing Project Open Hand today.

To meet the urgent need for food—and to make sure there is a regular supply of it on a daily basis—Open Hand has set up a special fund that will be used exclusively to feed people with AIDS.

It's called the 100% Food Fund—and every cent that goes into it will be used to purchase, prepare and deliver food.

Here in the Bay Area—which is known throughout the world for its cuisine—it's easy to forget just how basic and important food is. But for the people living with AIDS who depend on Project Open Hand, food isn't just basic—it's survival. For many of these people, meals and groceries from Open Hand mean the difference between eating and going hungry.

For all of them, the nutritious, appealing food they receive from Open Hand helps them keep up their weight—and their spirits—and enables them to better fight their illness and stand up to often drastic medical treatments.

Let me share some "food facts" with you, to give you a better picture of the enormous amount of food it takes to feed over 2,700 people with AIDS—and why your support of Open Hand is so urgently needed:

FACT #1—Every month the Open Hand kitchen goes through 7,000 lbs. of chicken, 1,000 lbs. of rice, 1,600 lbs. of pasta, 800 dozen eggs, hundreds of pounds of fresh produce, and much more.

FACT #2—The supplies in the Project Open Hand Food Bank's 4,000-square-foot (that's half a football field!) warehouse must be replenished <u>every two weeks</u>.

FACT #3—Open Hand's monthly bill for food alone averages $110,000, and it's always growing.

FACT #4—Even though Open Hand receives generous donations of food from individuals, restaurants, and food stores, <u>the organization still has to purchase 90% of the food used in its kitchen</u>.

The number of people who depend on Project Open Hand increases every day—which means that the amount of food needed also increases every day. The fact is, Open Hand can only be there for everyone in need with the help of people like you.

Project Open Hand has been feeding people with AIDS now for eight years. They tell me that every day they re-learn the same humbling lesson: <u>a hand extended to someone in need never comes back empty</u>.

I'm asking you to help Project Open Hand today, by making a special donation. Your donation will help Open Hand provide meals and groceries for the growing number of people living with AIDS. <u>It will be like a gift of food for people who urgently need it and greatly appreciate it</u>.

Over 1,900 people with AIDS count on an Open Hand volunteer to knock on their door and deliver a hot meal or a bag of groceries. Hundreds of other people with AIDS depend on the groceries they receive from the Project Open Hand Food Bank.

Altogether, over 2,700 people living with AIDS count on Project Open Hand to be there every day—which really means they are <u>depending on people like you</u>.

Will you help us feed those who need the proper sustenance to fight their disease, keep up their spirits and better tolerate often drastic medical treatments?

A donation of $35 to the 100% Food Fund will buy enough chicken to feed 80 people with AIDS. $70 will provide 112 portions of beef stew.

On behalf of all the people with AIDS who will receive meals with love as a result of your support, <u>I want to thank you</u>.

Sincerely,

Martin Yan
Yan Can Cook

P.S. Please help Open Hand win the battle against malnutrition for people with AIDS—send a contribution today!

PROJECT OPEN HAND 100% FOOD FUND

Dear Martin,
    I want to help make sure Open Hand can purchase all the food needed to provide meals and groceries to the growing number of people with AIDS. Enclosed is my donation to help Project Open Hand feed people with AIDS.

☐$35   ☐$70   ☐$100   ☐$200   ☐Other $_____

100% of your gift will go directly to buying, preparing and delivering the food Open Hand needs for the growing number of people with AIDS.

PLEASE MAKE ANY CORRECTIONS TO MAILING LABEL.

Please make check payable to Project Open Hand. Your donation is tax-deductible.

YOUR DONATION=FOOD=STRENGTH, SUSTENANCE & LOVE FOR PEOPLE WITH AIDS

☐ I would like to make my gift: ☐ in memory of: ☐ in honor of:

(PLEASE PRINT)

☐ Please send a card acknowledging my gift to:

Name_____

Address_____

_____

We're trying our best to avoid duplication in our mailings. If you're already a donor, or if you've received more than one copy of this mailing, please let us know.

PROJECT OPEN HAND ♥ 2720 17th STREET, SAN FRANCISCO, CALIFORNIA 94110 ♥ 415-558-0600

Thank you very much!

OPEN HAND

> **After You Read**

> **The pen is mightier than the sword.**
>
> **—BULWER-LYTTON**

About the Content

1. What is Project Open Hand?

2. What services does it provide?

3. What is funding used for?

4. How much of its food does Project Open Hand have to purchase?

5. How do the food deliveries help AIDS patients?

6. What is the 100% Food Fund?

About the Writing

1. How does the opening paragraph catch your attention?

2. Why has the writer used underlining?

3. Why has the letter come from Martin Yan, a chef with a popular cooking show on television, rather than the director of the organization?

4. What techniques does the writer use to convince you to donate money?

5. What is the purpose of the "shopping list" that was included?

6. What techniques are used on the contribution form?

Quickwrite

Write for 10 minutes on this topic: What organizations do you (or would you like to) give donations to? Why? How do they help the community?

ACADEMIC POWER STRATEGY

Apply the Strategy

Learn to work effectively in a group to help you with group work assigned in all your classes. College courses often ask students to work together in groups to prepare assignments. For some people, this is an exciting, enjoyable opportunity. Others have concerns about it: How will they be graded? How will the work be divided fairly? How can the group stay organized?

Organize a small group. Imagine that your group constitutes a new committee for Project Open Hand. Instead of appealing for money, however, you are appealing for volunteers. People are needed to cook and deliver meals. Your committee has to produce the following materials to send in a mass mailing to your community:

- a letter of appeal

- a volunteer sign-up form

- any other literature you think will be helpful

Use the information in the previous reading and the information on effective persuasive techniques to help you write your mailing. Show the materials your committee develops to your class. Whose materials would convince you to donate your time? Why? Discuss the projects with your class.

After you have finished, write an evaluation of your own committee. Answer these questions:

1. How well did each member cooperate with the group?

2. What problems did you encounter?

3. What are the strengths and weaknesses of your group?

Writing Tip: Three Parts of Persuasion

Persuasion is also important in academic writing. It can be used to defend an opinion or justify the analysis of data or other facts. In academic writing, persuasion typically contains three main elements, presented in this order in an essay:

1. **Background Information:** In order to build a convincing argument, you must tell your reader the facts of the case. These facts should be clear, documented, truthful, and support your main argument. For example, in a paper about homelessness, statistics regarding the number of homeless would probably be needed to support your argument.

2. **Concession:** Every argument has two sides. Although as a writer you may be defending one side of an argument, you need to show your readers that you have considered the opposing side's point of view. This is often called a concession. A **concession** demonstrates that you have taken into consideration the counterargument, but still believe your argument is stronger. For example, in an paper that argues for the elimination of grading at your school, you might *concede* that some students may do more poorly because they are motivated only by grades, but that overall, students will focus more on their work and not on the grade. However, a *false concession* merely states that there is another side: "While some students believe that grades should be eliminated, I believe they shouldn't." This "concession" doesn't *concede* anything; it merely states that there are two sides.

3. **The Appeal:** The appeal is the main part of the argument, in which you state what you believe and why the readers should believe it, too. Appeals can be subtle or bold, depending on the author's feelings about the subject matter. In the appeal, you should make it clear to the reader what you want him or her to do. For example, in an essay that addresses the problem of teenage runaways, you may appeal to your readers simply to be more sympathetic, or to take action in their communities by setting up homes for runaways.

◆**Getting Ready to Read**

The next reading argues that North Americans need to examine their habit of moving frequently. Do you think that North Americans are too mobile? Is that necessarily a bad thing?

◆**Vocabulary Check**

The words and phrases in this list are included in the reading. How many of them do you know? Check them. Look up the ones you don't know, or discuss them with a classmate. Then write a definition or an example sentence in your Vocabulary Log.

_____ blue-collar _____ corporate raider _____ increment

_____ bulldoze _____ frontiersman _____ privatization

_____ congenial _____ gentrification

Read

Reading 2: Rootlessness

by David Morris

1 Americans are a rootless people. Each year one in six of us changes residences; one in four changes jobs. We see nothing troubling in these statistics. For most of us, they merely reflect the restless energy that made America great. A nation of immigrants, unsurprisingly, celebrates those willing to pick up stakes and move on: the **frontiersman,** the cowboy, the entrepreneur, the **corporate raider.**

2 Rootedness has never been a goal of public policy in the United States. In the 1950s and 1960s local governments **bulldozed** hundreds of inner city neighborhoods, all in the name of urban renewal. In the 1960s and 1970s court-ordered busing[1] forced tens of thousands of children to abandon their neighborhood schools, all in the interest of racial harmony. In the 1980s a wave of hostile takeovers shuffled hundreds of billions of dollars of corporate assets, all in the pursuit of economic efficiency.

3 Hundreds of thousands of informal gathering spots that once nurtured community across the country have disappeared. The soda fountain and the lunch counter are gone. The branch library is an endangered species. Even the number of neighborhood taverns is declining. In the 1940s, 90 percent of beer and spirits was consumed in public places. Today only 30 percent is.

4 This **privatization** of American public life is most apparent to overseas visitors. "After four years here, I still feel more of a foreigner than in any other place in the world I have been," one well-traveled woman told Ray Oldenburg, the author of the marvelous book about public gathering spots, *The Great Good Place.* "There is no contact between the various households, we rarely see the neighbors and certainly do not know any of them."

5 The woman contrasts this with her life in Europe. "In Luxembourg, however, we would frequently stroll down to one of the local cafés in the evening and there pass a very **congenial** few hours in the company of the local fireman, dentist, bank employee, or whoever happened to be there at the time."

6 In most American cities, zoning laws prohibit mixing commerce and residence. The result is an overreliance on the car. Oldenburg cites the experience of a couple who had lived in a small house in Vienna and a large one in Los Angeles: "In Los Angeles we are hesitant to leave our sheltered home in order to visit friends or to participate in cultural or entertainment events because every such outing involves a major investment of time and nervous strain in driving long distances. In Vienna everything, opera, theaters, shops, cafés, are within easy walking distance."

7 Shallow roots weaken our ties in the neighborhood and workplace. The average **blue-collar** worker receives only seven days' notice before losing his or her job, only two days when not backed by a union. *The Whole Earth Review* unthinkingly echoes this lack of connectedness

---

[1]Court-ordered busing refers to a law that required that American schools be integrated. Since neighborhoods often were segregated, students would travel by bus to schools outside the areas in which they lived in order to achieve racial balance.

when it advises its readers to "first visit an electronics store near you and get familiar with the features—then compare price and shop mail order via [an] 800 number."[2]

8   This lack of connectedness breeds costly instability in American life. In business, when owners have no loyalty to workers, workers have no loyalty to owners. Quality of work suffers. Visiting Japanese management specialists point to our labor turnover rate as a key factor in our relative economic decline. In the pivotal electronics industry, for example, our turnover rate is four times that of Japan's.

9   American employers respond to declining sales and profit margins by cutting what they regard as their most expendable resource: employees. In Japan, corporate accounting systems consider labor a fixed asset. Japanese companies spend enormous amounts of money training workers. "They view that training as an investment, and they don't want to let the investment slip away," Martin K. Starr of Columbia University recently told *Business Week*. Twenty percent of the work force, the core workers in major industrial companies, have lifetime job security in Japan.

10   Rootlessness in the neighborhood also costs us dearly. Neighborliness saves money, a fact we often overlook because the transactions of strong, rooted neighborhoods take place outside of the money economy:

11   • Neighborliness reduces crime. People watch the streets where children play and know who the strangers are.

12   • Neighborliness saves energy. In the late 1970s Portland, Oregon, discovered it could save 5 percent of its energy consumption simply by reviving the corner grocery store. No longer would residents in need of a carton of milk or a loaf of bread have to drive to a shopping mall.

13   • Neighborliness lowers the cost of health care. "It is cruel and unusual punishment to send someone to a nursing home when they are not sick," says Dick Ladd, head of Oregon's Senior Services. But when we don't know our neighbors we can't rely on them. Society picks up the tab. Home-based care is one-quarter the cost of nursing home care.

14   Psychoanalyst and author Erich Fromm saw a direct correlation between the decline in the number of neighborhood bartenders and the rise in the number of psychiatrists. "Sometimes you want to go where everybody knows your name," goes the apt refrain of the popular TV show *Cheers*. Once you poured out your troubles over a nickel beer to someone who knew you and your family. And if you got drunk, well, you could walk home. Now you drive cross town and pay $100 an hour to a stranger for emotional relief.

15   The breakdown of community life may explain, in part, why the three best-selling drugs in America treat stress: ulcer medication (Tagamet), hypertension (Inderal), tranquilizer (Valium).

16   American society has evolved into a cultural environment where it is ever harder for deep roots to take hold. What can we do to change this?

17   • **Rebuild walking communities**. Teach urban planners that overdependence on transportation is a sign of failure in a social system. Impose the true costs of the car on its owners. Recent studies indicate that to do so would raise the cost of gasoline by as much as $2 a gallon. Recently Stockholm declared war on cars by imposing a $50 a month fee for car owners, promising to increase the fee until the city was given back to pedestrians and mass transit.

18   • **Equip every neighborhood with a library, a coffeehouse, a diversified shopping district, and a park.**

19   • **Make rootedness a goal of public policy.** In the 1970s a Vermont land use law, for

---

[2]In the United States, 800 numbers allow callers to dial long distance without a charge.

example, required an economic component to environmental impact statements. In at least one case, a suburban shopping mall was denied approval because it would undermine existing city businesses. In Berkeley, California, citizens voted two to one to permit commercial rent control in neighborhoods whose independently owned businesses were threatened by **gentrification.**

20   • **Reward stability and continuity.** Today, if a government seizes property it pays the owner the market price. Identical homes have identical value, even if one is home to a third-generation family, while the other is occupied by a new tenant. Why not pay a premium, say 50 percent above the current market price, for every 10 years the occupant has lived there? Forty years of residence would be rewarded with compensation four times greater than the market price. The **increment** above the market price should go not to the owner but to the occupant, if the two are not the same. By favoring occupants over owners, this policy not only rewards neighborliness, but promotes social justice. By raising the overall costs of dislocation, it also discourages development that undermines rootedness.

21   • **Prohibit hostile takeovers.** Japanese, German, and Swedish corporations are among the most competitive and innovative in

the world. But in these countries hostile takeovers are considered unethical business practices or are outlawed entirely.

22   • **Encourage local and employee ownership.** Protecting existing management is not the answer if that management is not locally rooted. Very few cities have an ongoing economic campaign to promote local ownership despite the obvious advantages to the community. Employee ownership exists in some form in more than 5,000 U.S. companies, but in only a handful is that ownership significant.

23   • **And above all, correct our history books.** America did not become a wealthy nation because of rootlessness, but in spite of it. A multitude of natural resources across an expansive continent and the arrival of tens of millions of skilled immigrants furnished us enormous advantages. We could overlook the high social costs of rootlessness. This is no longer true.

24   Instability is not the price we must pay for progress. Loyalty, in the plant and the neighborhood, does not stifle innovation. These are lessons we've ignored too long. More rooted cultures such as Japan and Germany are now outcompeting us in the marketplace, and in the neighborhood. We would do well to learn the value of community.

◆ After You Read

About the Content

1. List all the advantages that a sense of community gives to a nation, as explained by Morris.

2. Do you disagree with any of these points? Explain your answer.

3. What is Morris's main argument? Phrase it in a single sentence.

4. How would you characterize the neighborliness in your own community?

5. What do you think you could do in your own community to improve neighborliness?

About the Writing

1. In what ways does Morris use authority to support his argument? Find all the instances in this article.

2. How does Morris use persuasive writing to convey his point?

3. Does Morris commit any logical fallacies or weaknesses in persuasion?

4. Why does Morris repeat the word "neighborliness" in paragraphs 10–13? What effect does it have on the writing?

5. Morris makes a subtle concession. Can you identify it?

6. Restate Morris's appeal in your own words.

Quickwrite:

Write for 10 minutes on this topic: Have you ever lived in a neighborhood or community that was very close-knit? What was that experience like?

FROM READING TO WRITING

You have read persuasive arguments in this chapter. In both cases, these arguments have attempted to show you why a certain cause or idea is important, and why you should believe them or act upon them. As you write your own paper, think about the elements of persuasive writing you have learned, and try to apply them.

◆Getting Ready to Write

For this essay, you will again develop your own writing topic. The subject for the paper is *one of your community's most important problems.* In your essay, you should provide facts about the situation, using information from appropriate authorities (interviews, readings, or whatever is fitting). In addition, you should convince your reader why this is an important problem and what might be done to correct it.

Use the invention techniques explained in Chapter 1, such as brainstorming and freewriting, to decide on a topic that interests you. Make a list of all the problems that exist in your community (your community could be your community back home, your school community—however you want to define it). Then select a topic. Recall the triangle presented in the last chapter. Fill in the following triangle with your topic and thesis.

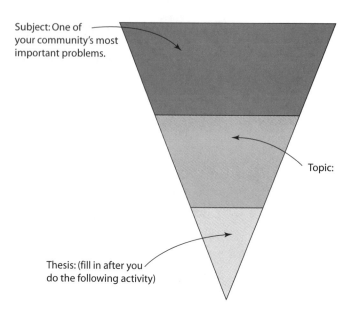

Subject: One of your community's most important problems.

Topic:

Thesis: (fill in after you do the following activity)

Writing Tip: Reviewing Thesis Statements

Work with a group of classmates to determine which of the following statements are good thesis statements and which are not. Be prepared to explain your decisions to your class.

1. Homelessness is a problem in my community.

2. Family problems cause many teenagers to become dangerously depressed.

3. At the university, cheating on examinations is common.

4. Inadequate public transportation contributes to isolation of the elderly.

5. Competition for high grades causes a breakdown in friendships at our school.

    Now, write a *draft thesis statement* (it doesn't have to be perfect). Put your thesis statement into the triangle above. With a partner, discuss the following questions for your thesis statement:

- Is it arguable?

- Is it a single sentence?

- Is it interesting?

- Is there enough information to support it?

> **The sounder your argument, the more satisfaction you get out of it.**
>
> **—ED HOWE**

- Is it grammatical?

- Is it specific? (That is, does it make only one point?)

After your discussion, make any changes to your thesis statement that you think are necessary.

When you have formulated a good thesis, assemble the materials you will need to begin the drafting process. These include:

- Notes from your reading and class discussion

- Relevant quickwrite topics

- Notes on personal experience that you want to include

- Quotations from your reading that support your thesis

- Facts or information from "experts" or other people whose opinions are important

 Write

Review the instructions on writing a first draft in the previous chapter. You are now ready to write your first draft.

After You Write

Revise

Exchange drafts with a partner. Read your drafts carefully, and answer the following questions thoroughly:

1. Is the title effective and interesting? Explain.

2. How effective is the introduction? Does it explain the issue? Does it have a thesis that is clear and arguable?

3. What is the writer's argument? Restate his or her main appeal in your own words.

4. Does the writer provide adequate background information? What would you still like to know about the subject, in order to be convinced?

5. What concessions does the writer make? Are they effective? Explain.

6. Is the paper well organized? Are transitions used effectively?

7. Does the conclusion end the paper effectively?

8. What other problems do you see in this paper?

Discuss your answers with your partner.

Remember that revision is not merely correcting your spelling and grammar, and inserting a few commas. In the revision phase of the writing process, you are reorganizing, cutting, adding detail, and improving your choices. Looking at the review you received from your partner and your response to it, formulate a revision plan. Use the following chart to help you identify the areas that need the most improvement.

Feature	Problem	Possible Solution
Title		
Opening paragraph		
Examples		
Organization		
Word choice		
Conclusion		
Wordiness		
Other		

Use your revision plan to guide your rewriting.

◇ Grammar You Can Use: Eliminating Wordiness

Effective sentences use exactly the right number of words necessary to get their message across. There is no magic number, however. Charles Dickens's *Tale of Two Cities* starts with a sentence that is 128 words long, yet it is considered a masterpiece:

> It was the best of times, it was the worst of times, it was the age of wisdom, it was the age of foolishness, it was the epoch of belief, it was the epoch of incredulity, it was the season of Light, it was the season of Darkness, it was the spring of hope, it was the winter of despair, we had everything before us, we had nothing before us, we were all going direct to Heaven, we were all going direct the other way—in short, the period was so far like the present period, that some of its noisiest authorities insisted on being received, for good or for evil, in the superlative degree of comparison only.

Moby Dick begins with a three-word sentence, and is also considered a masterpiece:

> "Call me Ishmael."

Ultimately, you will need to decide when you have a sentence that is the right number of words. Here are five principles for improving the conciseness of your writing:

1. Eliminate redundant words. (Redundant words are underlined in this example. What makes them redundant?)

   Example: <u>Currently,</u> what we need <u>now</u> is a <u>novel</u> new plan.

   Revised: What we need is a new plan.

2. Eliminate "empty" words. (Replace them with simpler words with the same meaning.)

   at this point in time = now

   at that point in time = then

   at this juncture = now

   at the present time = now

   in a relatively short amount of time = quickly

   (and many more!)

3. Eliminate weak modifiers. If you use any of the following words, check to be sure they add essential information to the sentence. If not, replace them with a more precise word, or get rid of them altogether:

   really, very, definitely, quite, awfully, fine, nice, just,

   Example: He is really a very tall man.

   Revised: He is seven feet tall.
      He is very tall.

Cartoon by Bill Watterson, © 1994 Andrews and McMeel, a Universal Press Syndicate Company.

4. Replace wordy phrases.

   Example: When she was trying to find her new book, she seemed quite upset. She had just bought it recently.

   Revision: She seemed upset while trying to find her new book, because she had just bought it.

5. Simplify sentence structures; use adjectives.

   Example: Pearl, who was a teacher, wanted to take a vacation in Hawaii.

   Revision: Pearl, a teacher, wanted a Hawaiian vacation.

6. Eliminate "it is . . . that" structures.

   Example: It is the state of Washington that is most famous for apple production.

   Revision: The state of Washington is most famous for apple production.

7. Minimize the number of prepositional phrases per sentence.

   Example: The members <u>of</u> the committee <u>for</u> which I am the leader want to form a subcommittee devoted <u>to</u> the restructuring <u>of</u> the entire organization <u>of</u> our club.

   Revision: The committee, of which I am the leader, wants to form a subcommittee to restructure our club's organization.

8. Reduce unnecessary nominalizations.

   Nominalization refers to taking a perfectly good verb and turning it into a noun. Structures that rely on nominalization frequently rely too much on the verb <u>to be</u> as well, making for weak writing.

   Example: My <u>realization</u> of my <u>procrastination</u> is an <u>alteration</u> in my thinking.

   Revision: I realized that I procrastinate, which has altered my thinking.

Practice

Make the following sentences more concise.

1. It is not completely impossible, at the present time, to begin to develop an ample supply of monetary resources.

   _____

   _____

> We hardly find any persons of good sense save those who agree with us.
>
> —FRANÇOIS DE LA ROCHEFOUCAULD

2. Each individual person in attendance should obtain the approval of his or her personal instructor before leaving the classroom area.

_____

_____

3. Three of my very closest friends just want to go to the party, but I much prefer a movie for the evening's entertainment.

_____

_____

4. Excuse me, but would you mind terribly much, if it's not too much trouble, opening the window just a very little?

_____

_____

5. My grandmother is eighty-six years of age, but she has the capability of dancing the night away, just like people who are thirty years her junior in age.

_____

_____

6. It was the assistance of the three women that was of great importance to our organization.

_____

_____

Self-Correction:

In a recent piece of writing, identify areas where you had difficulty with wordiness. Rewrite any sentences that were too wordy.

Edit

After you have solved the problems identified in your revision plan, you can focus on editing and proofreading your paper. The editing phase includes double-checking your grammar, spelling, punctuation, and so forth. Each student has unique problems in this area, so it may be helpful to take an inventory of problem spots, based on your past experience as a writer. Remember, you can change this inventory as you progress.

Which of the items shown on the next page do you think are a problem for you? Check the appropriate column.

PROBLEM	MAJOR PROBLEM	MINOR PROBLEM	NO PROBLEM	DON'T KNOW
Spelling	_____	_____	_____	_____
Punctuation	_____	_____	_____	_____
Subject–verb agreement	_____	_____	_____	_____
Verb tenses	_____	_____	_____	_____
Articles	_____	_____	_____	_____
Prepositions	_____	_____	_____	_____
Plurals	_____	_____	_____	_____
Sentence fragments	_____	_____	_____	_____
Run-on sentences	_____	_____	_____	_____
Wordiness	_____	_____	_____	_____
Transitions	_____	_____	_____	_____
Parallel structures	_____	_____	_____	_____

If you have checked more than three as a "major problem," decide which three you would like to work on first. It's easier to concentrate on a few problem areas at a time.

The last step should be proofreading—that is, looking for careless mistakes: misspellings, leaving out words, typing words twice in a row, and so forth. Before you turn your paper in, proofread it carefully.

PUTTING IT ALL TOGETHER

Arguments are, by nature, controversial. What issues matter to you? Help organize discussions or debates on topics you choose.

Begin by brainstorming with your classmates on issues that matter to you. Consult with your teacher about the topics. (Note that certain topics, such as those that involve religion or politics, are often *ineffective* debate topics because people usually will not be persuaded to abandon their beliefs.)

To organize your debate, at least three people should represent each side of the argument. Prepare notes in advance. Organize the time as follows:

Side 1: Opening statement: 2 minutes
Side 2: Opening statement: 2 minutes
Side 1: Main argument: 3 minutes
Side 2: Main argument: 3 minutes
Side 1: Rebuttal: 3 minutes
Side 2: Rebuttal: 3 minutes

Side 1: Closing argument: 2 minutes
Side 2: Closing argument: 2 minutes

After the debate, the class should vote anonymously on who they think won the debate. Be sure to base your vote on which side argued more effectively, *not* on which side you agree with.

Test-Taking Tip

Reducing your anxiety about taking tests will help you become a more effective test-taker. If you are feeling anxious about an upcoming test, you can relax a little by writing in your journal. Here are some ideas of what to write about:

- Make a list of the ten things you like to do most. Choose one or two things on the list that you find extremely pleasant. Describe them in detail.

- Think about your greatest success in school. Write about how you felt when you did well.

- Write about the most relaxing place you know: a lake, a tree house, your favorite café, etc. Write about how you feel when you are there.

Writing about pleasant memories will help you relax and take the focus off your anxiety.

CHECK YOUR PROGRESS

On a scale of 1 to 5, rate how well you have mastered the goals set at the beginning of the chapter:

1 2 3 4 5   examine writing for important features you have learned.

1 2 3 4 5   understand common problems/pitfalls in persuasive writing.

1 2 3 4 5   work effectively in a group.

1 2 3 4 5   eliminate wordiness in your writing.

1 2 3 4 5   (your own goal) _____

1 2 3 4 5   (your own goal) _____

If you've given yourself a 3 or lower on any of these goals:

- visit the *Tapestry* web site for additional practice.

- ask your instructor for extra help.

- review the sections of the chapter that you found difficult.

- work with a partner or study group to further your progress.

L ook closely at the photo, and then discuss these questions with your classmates:

- What are the people in this photo doing?
- What kind of writing do you think businesspeople do in their careers?
- What kind of writing do you think scientists do in their careers?
- Are you interested in pursuing a business or science career?

PROPOSING: THE SCIENCE OF BUSINESS, THE BUSINESS OF SCIENCE

10

The worlds of business and science thrive on communication—memos, e-mail, letters, proposals, and reports are all critical to success in these fields. This chapter introduces you to writing appropriately for science and business.

Setting Goals

In this chapter you will explore written communication in the worlds of business and science. In this chapter, you will learn how to:

◈ understand and use proper writing formats in workplace communication.

◈ understand the appropriate types of address required in business writing.

◈ consider your career options early to help you choose the right courses in school.

◈ use rules to avoid mistakes in spelling.

What other goals do you have for learning about workplace writing? Write two more here.

_____

_____

187

Getting Started

Before you begin the chapter, take a few minutes to write down what you know about workplace writing. You can begin by answering these questions:

1. What is a memo?

2. Why is format important in business communication?

3. What is a proposal?

LANGUAGE LEARNING STRATEGY

Understand and use proper writing formats in workplace communication to succeed in your communication goals. Different kinds of business communication require different formats: short memos, long letters, reports, brochures, and many others. Choosing the right format for business communication will help make it more effective.

Apply the Strategy

Collect examples of business communication. Here are some sources for business communication:

1. Look at advertising letters in the mail.

2. Get brochures or reports from your bank or college.

3. Ask friends or relatives for examples of business correspondence.

Bring one or two samples to class. As a group, look at the samples.

- Can you put them into categories?

- What formats do they use?

- What other features do you notice about them?

Getting Ready to Read

Memos and letters are important types of business correspondence. Memos are usually written *within* a company; letters are sent to people *outside* the writer's company. Here are samples showing how to format and write memos and letters. There are alternative ways to format these kinds of communication, but these general formats will be acceptable in nearly any situation.

Read   **Reading 1: Sample Memo Format**

Your Company Name
Your Company Address

To: Tapestry Readers (Recipient of Memo)
From: MES (memo writer's name or initials)
Subject: Sample Memo (title of memo in initial capitals)
Date: (date of memo)

People read business memos quickly. Therefore, you should get to the point in the first paragraph. If possible, get to the point in the first sentence.

Single-space your memos, and skip a line between paragraphs. Space your memo on the page so that it does not crowd the top or bottom of the paper.

Keep the sentence and paragraph lengths fairly short for memos that make requests or announcements. Sentences should have fewer than twenty words, on average, and paragraphs fewer than seven lines. The entire memo should not take more than one page.

For memos that are short reports, slightly different rules apply. You can include sections for a summary, introduction, discussion, and conclusion. You also include a list of references at the end. In short-report memos, you can use headings and subheadings. You might also include illustrations, glossaries, and attachments (additional documents that you think the reader might need).

Send copies to anyone who would be directly affected by the memo.

The final paragraph should tell your readers what you want them to do or what you will do for them.

Attachments: (short description of extra documents)
cc: (name of person who will receive a copy of the memo)

Reading 2: Sample Letter Format

Your Company Name
Your Company Address

Date of Letter

Recipient's name
Recipient's title
Recipient's company
Recipient's company address
Recipient's Name:

People read business letters quickly. Therefore, you should get to the point in the first paragraph. If possible, get to the point in the first sentence.

Single-space your letters, and skip a line between paragraphs. Space your letter on the page so that it does not crowd the top or bottom of the paper.

Keep the sentence and paragraph lengths fairly short for letters that make requests or announcements. Sentences should have fewer than twenty words, on average, and paragraphs fewer than seven lines. The entire letter should not take more than one or two pages.

For letters that are short reports, slightly different rules apply. You can include sections for a summary, introduction, discussion, and conclusion. You also include a list of references at the end. In short-report letters, you can use headings and subheadings. You might also include illustrations, glossaries, and enclosures (additional documents that you think the reader might need).

Send copies to anyone who would be directly affected by the letter.

The final paragraph should tell your readers what you want them to do or what you will do for them.

Sincerely,

Signature
Name

Enclosures: (short description of extra documents)
cc: (name of person who will receive a copy of the letter)

After You Read

LANGUAGE LEARNING STRATEGY

Understand the appropriate types of address required in business writing. When writing business correspondence, what is the proper way to address the person to whom you are writing? This depends on a number of factors: 1) how well you know the person, 2) whether you know the person's professional status, and 3) what the norms of the profession are.

When you don't know who you are writing to, it is easy to mistakenly address a woman as "Mr." or a man as "Ms." Here are some brief guidelines to addressing people properly in business correspondence:

- When in doubt, use someone's full name: Dear Chris Smith, rather than "Dear Mr. Smith." (Chris could be the name of either a man or a woman.)

- If you have a personal relationship with the person, or he or she signs his letters with a first name only, it *might* be all right to address him or her by a first name. But, if you have any doubt, be more formal and use the full name.

- Don't use "Mrs." Or "Miss" unless you are *certain* that the woman to whom you are writing prefers it. "Ms." is the more commonly accepted form of address for women, as it applies to either a married or an unmarried woman.

- If you are addressing a professor or doctor, use "Prof." or "Dr."

Apply the Strategy

Write a salutation line (the line in the letter that states "Dear _____")
for a business letter to each of these people:

1. Pat Morales, a customer who requested information from your company

   Dear _____

2. Gina Davidson, a doctor at a local hospital whom you met briefly at a party

   Dear _____

(continued on next page)

3. Chris Terney, a professor at the university

Dear _____

4. Fred Frank, the president of another business. You know him well.

Dear _____

Getting Ready to Read

Another type of workplace writing is a proposal—a business proposal, research proposal, and so forth. The next reading is a research proposal written by a student. Notice the format that he uses for his proposal.

Vocabulary Check

The words and phrases in this list are included in the reading. Check the ones that you know. Look up the ones you don't, or discuss them with a classmate. Then write a definition or example sentence in your Vocabulary Log.

_____ appreciable	_____ imminent	_____ precursor
_____ culminate	_____ influx	_____ radon
_____ death toll	_____ magnitude	_____ resistivity
_____ devastate	_____ milestone	_____ seismology
_____ fault (geological)	_____ out of commission	_____ writhing

Read

Reading 3: A Proposal to Review How Geophysical Precursors Can Help Predict Earthquakes

by Christopher Gray

Introduction

1 Throughout the world, devastating earthquakes occur with little or no advance warning. Some of these earthquakes kill hundreds of people. If the times, **magnitudes,** and locations of these earthquakes could be accurately predicted, many lives could be saved. This document proposes a review of how monitoring geophysical[1] **precursors** can help in the short-term prediction of earthquakes. The proposed review will discuss the physical principles behind the monitoring of three common precursors and evaluate how accurate each

[1] **geophysical:** the composition of geological features.

monitoring is in predicting earthquakes. Included in this proposal are my methods for gathering information, a schedule for completing the review, and my qualifications.

Justification of Proposed Review

2   On the morning of April 18, 1906, the population of San Francisco was awakened by violent shaking and by the roar caused by the **writhing** and collapsing of buildings [Hodgson, 1964]. The ground appeared to be thrown into waves that twisted railways and broke the pavement into great cracks. Many buildings collapsed, while others were severely damaged. The earthquake caused fires in fifty or more points throughout the city. Fire stations were destroyed, alarms were put **out of commission,** and water mains were broken. As a result, the fires quickly spread throughout the city and continued for three days. The fires destroyed a 5 square-mile section at the heart of the city [Mileti and Fitzpatrick, 1993]. Even more disastrous was the Kwanto earthquake in Japan that **devastated** the cities of Yokohama and Tokyo on September 1, 1923 [Hodgson, 1993]. In Yokohama, over 50 percent of the buildings were destroyed [Bolt, 1993], and as many as 208 fires broke out and spread through the city [Hodgson, 1964]. When the disaster was over, 33,000 people were dead [Bolt, 1993]. In Tokyo, the damage from the earthquake was less, but the resulting fires were more devastating. The fires lasted three days and destroyed 40 percent of the city [Hodgson, 1964]. After the fire, 68,000 people were dead and 1 million people were homeless [Bolt, 1993].

3   Some earthquakes have been successfully predicted. One of the most famous predictions was the Haicheng Prediction in China. In 1970, Chinese scientists targeted the Liaoning Province as a site with potential for a large earthquake. These scientists felt that an earthquake would occur there in 1974 or 1975. On December 20, 1974, an earthquake warning

was issued. Two days later, a magnitude 4.8 earthquake struck the Liaoning Province; however, further monitoring suggested a larger earthquake was **imminent** [Mileti and others, 1981]. On February 4, 1975, the Chinese issued a warning that an earthquake would strike Haicheng within 24 hours [Bolt, 1993]. The people in Haicheng were evacuated, and about 5.5 hours later, a magnitude 7.3 earthquake shook the city of Haicheng. If the people hadn't been evacuated, the **death toll** could have exceeded 100,000.

4   Using geophysical precursors, the Chinese have predicted more than ten earthquakes with magnitudes greater than 5.0 [Meyer, 1977]. For example, the Chinese predicted a pair of earthquakes of magnitude 6.9 that occurred 97 minutes apart in Yunnan on May 19, 1976 [Bolt, 1993].

Objectives

5   I propose to review the available literature on how geophysical precursors can be used for short-term predictions of earthquakes. In this review, I will achieve the following three goals:

1. explain three commonly monitored geophysical precursors: ground uplift and tilt, increases in **radon** emissions, and changes in the electrical **resistivity** of rocks;
2. show what happens to each of these precursors during the five stages of an earthquake; and
3. discuss how each of these precursors is used for short-term earthquake predictions.

6   Geophysical precursors are changes in the physical state of the earth that are precursory to earthquakes. In addition to monitoring geophysical precursors, there are other strategies for predicting earthquakes—in particular, analyzing statistical data on prior earthquakes. Analyzing statistical data on prior earthquakes, however, is solely a long-term prediction technique [Bolt, 1993]. For that reason, I will not consider it.

7   In my review, I will discuss three common geophysical precursors: ground uplift and tilt, increases in radon emissions, and changes in the electrical resistivity of rocks. Earthquakes occur in five stages as there is a build up of elastic strain within **faults** in the earth, followed by the development of cracks in the rocks, then the **influx** of water into those cracks. The fourth stage is the actual rupture of the fault and the release of seismic waves. The fifth stage is the sudden drop in stress in the fault. In this stage, aftershocks occur.

8   During these five stages, the geophysical precursors follow distinct patterns. For instance, the ground uplift and tilt increases during the second stage as the volume of rock increases. In my review, I will relate how the three geophysical precursors relate to the five stages of an earthquake and how well this relation can be used to predict the oncoming fault rupture.

Plan of Action

9   This section presents my plan for obtaining the objectives discussed in the previous section. Because of the recent earthquakes in California and Japan, there has arisen a strong interest to predict earthquakes precisely. As a consequence of that strong interest, many books and journals have been written on earthquakes and earthquake prediction. I have gathered five books and several articles on the subject. In addition, there are dozens of books and articles available in the library. These books and articles should provide sufficient information for me to write my review. The following paragraphs discuss how I will use these sources in my research.

10   The first goal of my research is to explain the physical principles behind monitoring geophysical precursors. For example, why does the electrical resistivity of rocks decrease before an oncoming earthquake? Or, what does a sudden increase in radon emissions reveal about the future likelihood of a massive earthquake? The second goal of my research is to show what happens to each of these precursors during the five stages of an earthquake. To achieve these two goals, I will rely on three books that give an overview to earthquake prediction: *Earthquakes* [Bolt, 1988], *Earthquakes and Geological Discovery* [Bolt, 1993], and *Earthquakes and Earth Structure* [Hodgson, 1964].

11   A third primary goal of the literature review is to cover the accuracy of monitoring each precursor. By accuracy, I mean how well does the method work in predicting the time, place, and size of earthquakes. This discussion will not include many statistics on the predictions of earthquakes, because at present there just haven't been enough successful predictions to validate these types of statistics. Instead, I intend to evaluate the potential accuracy of monitoring each precursor based on the opinions of experts and preliminary data. To achieve this goal, I will rely on two of my most recent sources: *The Great Earthquake Experiment* [Mileti and Fitzpatrick, 1993] and *Earthquakes and Geological Discovery* [Bolt, 1993].

12   Should I require additional sources other than the ones I have, I will search for them in the library system at the University of Wisconsin. Should I not be able to find that information, I will modify the scope of my research accordingly.

13   Because the primary readers for my proposed literature review are engineering students who are probably not familiar with the theories behind earthquakes, I will have to provide selected background information from my sources. These engineering students already know that earthquakes are devastating. They also know that if earthquakes could be predicted, people would be able to prepare for them and lives would be saved. However, they may not know the different methods of predicting earthquakes. My intent is to inform these students of three methods of predicting earthquakes.

14   A secondary audience for the review would be non-technical readers who either live in earthquake-prone areas or are affected finan-

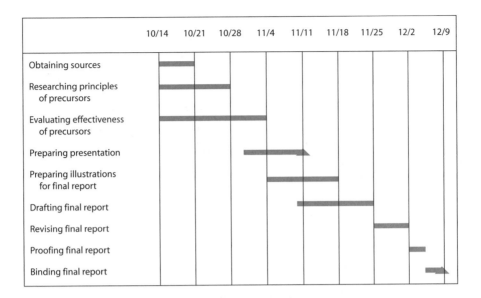

	10/14	10/21	10/28	11/4	11/11	11/18	11/25	12/2	12/9
Obtaining sources									
Researching principles of precursors									
Evaluating effectiveness of precursors									
Preparing presentation									
Preparing illustrations for final report									
Drafting final report									
Revising final report									
Proofing final report									
Binding final report									

Figure 1. Schedule for completion of literature review. The two triangles represent milestones **for the project, the first being the formal presentation on November 11, 1996, and the second being the formal report on December 9, 1996.**

cially when earthquakes occur. My proposed literature review will provide this group with an unbiased discussion of three methods for earthquake prediction. This discussion, drawing much from overview chapters in *Earthquakes, Animals and Man* [Deshpande, 1987] and *California Quake* [Meyer, 1977], will put into perspective how accurate, or inaccurate, the named methods are and what hurdles face engineers who try to predict earthquakes.

Management Plan

15   This section presents my schedule, costs, and qualifications for performing the proposed research. The proposed research project **culminates** in a formal report that will be completed by December 6, 1995. To reach this goal, I will follow the schedule presented in Figure 1. Because I already possess several books and articles on earthquake prediction, most of my time will be spent sifting through the information,

finding the key results, and presenting those results to the audience.

16   Given that I can obtain all my sources for the literature review from the library, there is no **appreciable** cost associated with performing this literature review. The only costs, which will be minor, are for copying articles, printing the review, and spiral binding the review. I estimate that I can do these tasks for under $10.

17   I am a senior in the Geological Engineering Department at the University of Wisconsin at Madison. In my undergraduate courses I have taken rock mechanics, soil mechanics, geophysics, and stratigraphy, all of which have included the principles of **seismology** and stress–strain relationships. In addition, I have taken field courses on structural geology that have introduced me to subsurface behaviors. I believe that these courses and my hands-on experience will aid me in assimilating the proposed literature review. For further information about my qualifications, see the attached résumé.[*]

*The résumé is not included here.

References

....

18 Bolt, Bruce A., *Earthquakes* (New York: W. H. Freeman and Company, 1988).

Bolt, Bruce A., *Earthquakes and Geological Discovery* (New York: Scientific American Library, 1993).

Deshpande, Prof. B. G., *Earthquakes, Animals and Man* (Pune, India: The Maharashtra Association for the Cultivation of Science, 1987).

Hodgson, John H., *Earthquakes and Earth Structure* (Englewood Cliffs, NJ: Prentice-Hall, 1964).

Meyer, Larry L., *California Quake* (Nashville: Sherbourne Press, 1977).

Mileti, Dennis S., and Colleen Fitzpatrick, *The Great Earthquake Experiment* (Boulder, CO: Westview Press, 1993).

◆ After You Read

About the Content

1. What were two of the most devastating earthquakes, according to Gray?

2. What is the main purpose of his research proposal?

3. Which earthquakes have been successfully predicted?

4. What are the author's three goals in his research?

5. What are the author's qualifications to carry out the research?

About the Writing

1. How does the researcher justify the need for his research? How does he provide evidence?

2. Who are the intended audiences for his research? How does the researcher identify them?

3. How would you characterize the level of formality of this proposal?

4. Describe the organization of the proposal.

5. Why do you think he includes the graphic of his schedule? Do you think this is a good idea?

© CNN

TUNING IN: "Summer Jobs"

....

Watch the CNN video about summer jobs. Discuss these questions with your class:

- What should applicants do if they want a summer job?

- What kinds of summer jobs are available?

- What did you learn about getting a job?

In your journal, respond to this question:

• What is the ideal summer job, in your opinion?

FROM READING TO WRITING

You have learned about different types of business writing in this chapter. These examples have shown you the importance of formats, and ways to keep your writing focused and clear.

As you begin the writing assignment, remember the techniques you have learned in this chapter.

Getting Ready to Write

> I have made this letter longer than usual, because I lack the time to make it short.
>
> —BLAISE PASCAL

For this paper, you will write a proposal for a project you would like to complete. This proposal can be done with a partner or committee, or by yourself. Your proposal can address research you would like to complete or a business project you would like to undertake. If you have a project in mind, you can use your topic. Or you can brainstorm with a group of classmates.

Write a list of ten business or research proposals you might be interested in doing. One is done for you as an example. Then eliminate those that are less interesting or seem too difficult to undertake. Write your list here:

Starting an on-campus delivery service
_____
_____
_____
_____
_____
_____
_____
_____
_____

Write

After you have chosen your topic, complete the following outline (refer to the section beginning on page 192 if you don't understand any part of the following outline):

Title: A Proposal . . . _____

Author: _____

1. Introduction

2. Justification of proposed study/project

3. Objectives

4. Plan of action

5. Management plan

6. References

> To write what is worth publishing, to find honest people to publish it, and get sensible people to read it, are the three great difficulties in being an author.
>
> **—CHARLES CALEB COLTON**

Finish by writing a cover letter, summarizing the proposal and stating why you think it's an important one.

ACADEMIC POWER STRATEGY

Consider your career options early to help you choose the right courses while you are in school. Although it is not necessary to know exactly what your major will be the day you enter college, it is important to consider what careers you might be interested in pursuing. Most colleges offer lots of opportunities to explore your career choices.

Apply the Strategy

Complete the following information. Work with a partner to see how much of the information you can find.

1. Does your school have a career counseling office? Where is it?

   _____

2. Does your school sponsor a job fair, where employers distribute information about their companies? When and where will this job fair take place?

   _____

3. What books are available in your library about choosing a career?

   _____

4. What student organizations with a career focus exist on your campus? (for example, a business club, a pre-med club)

   _____

5. What other resources are available on your campus for career planning or development?

   _____

After You Write

Revise

Give your draft to a classmate or to another group if you have worked in a committee. Ask your reader(s) for specific feedback on your proposal. Ask your reader(s) to answer these questions:

1. Did the writer follow the proposal outline clearly?

2. Was the explanation of the project clear in the introduction?

3. Are the plan of action and management of the project reasonable?

4. Are the references included useful? Do you have other suggestions for resource material?

5. Is the author qualified to undertake the proposed study or project?

Now complete the following table, as you did in the previous chapters. Use your revision plan to guide your rewriting.

Feature	Problem	Possible Solution
Title		
Follow the outline		
Word choice		
Documentation and references		
Other		

(Also, refer to page 38 of Chapter 2 for help in revising your draft.)

Grammar You Can Use: Spelling Rules

The complex history of the English language has contributed to many spelling irregularities. There are a few rules that can help you (see below), but there are also many exceptions to these spelling rules. Fortunately, there are now some helpful tools for fixing poor spelling; computer spell-checkers and electronic dictionaries can take some of the work out of looking words up.

A good strategy is to keep records of words you frequently misspell. Create a section in your journal or notebook. It's also smart to note new words from your reading that you think you would probably misspell. When you misspell a word, look up the correct spelling and write it down. It helps to write it several times, and to look at it carefully. Research shows that good spellers recognize the *shape* of words, the way they look on the page, and not just spelling rules. If you confuse two words that sound alike, write their definitions as well.

Ten spelling rules

1. Doubling consonants: When adding *-ed, -ing,* or *-y* to one-syllable words whose preceding vowel is "short," double the final consonants:

   (bet, betting).

   Don't double consonants when the vowel sound is "long:"

   (beat, beating).

2. Plurals: With regular plurals, add *-es* when a word ends in *-s, -ch, -sh, -x,* or *-z* (*boxes, torches, bushes*). Most words that end

in -*y* change to -*ie* before adding -*s* (*tally, tallies; baby, babies*), but words that end in -*ey*, -*ay*, or -*oy* do not (*holiday, holidays; turkey, turkeys*).

3. *i* before *e*: A rule that most English speakers learn and believe is:

I before *e*,

except after *c*,

or when sounded like *a*,

as in *neighbor* or *weigh*.

Although this works for a small set of words, there are many exceptions, including *weird, neither, science, glacier, either*, and dozens of others.

4. -*able* or -*ible*: There are more words that end in -*able* than -*ible*, so if you aren't sure, go with -*able*. After a complete word, it's usually -*able*; after a word that ends in -*miss (permissible)* or an incomplete word that ends in a "soft" *g* sound (*eligible*), it's usually -*ible*.

5. Drop final -*e*: When you add an ending to a word that ends in -*e*, and the ending begins with a consonant, keep the final -*e* (*sore, sorely*). In other cases, drop the final -*e* (*hope, hoping*).

6. *y* or *i*: A word that ends in -*y* changes the -*y* to *i* before -*ness* or -*ly* (*happy, happiness*). A word that ends in -*ie* changes the -*ie* to -*y* before adding -*ing* (*lie, lying*).

7. -*c* or -*ck*: A word that ends in a "hard" -*c* adds a -*k* before an ending that begins with a vowel (*picnic, picnicking*).

8. -*ful* or -*full*: The suffix is always -*ful*, never -*full* (*handful, beautiful*). When you add the ending -*ly*, then you have two *l*'s (*thankful, thankfully*).

9. -*sede*, -*ceed*, or -*cede*: *Supersede* is the only common English word that ends in -*sede*. *Exceed, succeed*, and *proceed* are the only common words that end in -*ceed*. The ending for other words is -*cede* (*precede, intercede*).

10. -*ery* or -*ary*: Only five commonly used English words end in -*ery*: *stationery* (writing paper), *cemetery, monastery, distillery*, and *confectionery*. The rest end in -*ary*.

There are lists of commonly misused, misspelled, and confused words in Appendix 1 on page 206.

> A memorandum is written not to inform the reader but to protect the writer.
>
> —DEAN GOODERHAM ACHESON

Practice

Find the mistakes in the following sentences. Explain your answers. Not all sentences have errors.

1. I have a feelling that a storm is about to develope.

2. It was such an embarassing arguement—wether soccer is better than football—who cares?

3. His adress is fourty-four Independance Avenue, near the cemetary.

4. He garantees his morgage will be payed on time.

5. The Library League meets the first Wednesday in February.

6. It is neccessary to protect our fragile enviroment.

7. In order to suceed in your freight business, you must aquaint yourself with all the tarriff and license regulations.

8. The cheif justice of the Eighth Circiut Court handed down her judgment.

9. The physician reccomends that the elderly be vacinnated against pneumonia.

10. I allready have a reciept for the new matress.

Self-Correction

In your essay, identify areas where you had difficulty with incorrectly spelled words. Copy any sentences with errors in them; then rewrite each sentence correctly.

Edit

After you have solved the problems identified in your revision plan, you can focus on editing and proofreading your paper. The editing phase includes double-checking your grammar, spelling, punctuation, and so forth. Each student has unique problems in this area, so it may be helpful to take an inventory of problem spots, based on your past experience as a writer. Remember, you can change this inventory as you progress.

Which of the following items do you think are a problem for you? Check the appropriate column.

PROBLEM	MAJOR PROBLEM	MINOR PROBLEM	NO PROBLEM	DON'T KNOW
Spelling	_____	_____	_____	_____
Punctuation	_____	_____	_____	_____
Subject–verb agreement	_____	_____	_____	_____
Verb tenses	_____	_____	_____	_____
Articles	_____	_____	_____	_____
Prepositions	_____	_____	_____	_____
Plurals	_____	_____	_____	_____
Sentence fragments	_____	_____	_____	_____
Run-on sentences	_____	_____	_____	_____
Wordiness	_____	_____	_____	_____
Parallel structures	_____	_____	_____	_____

If you have checked more than three as a "major problem," decide which three you would like to work on first. It's easier to concentrate on a few problem areas at a time.

The last step should be proofreading—that is, looking for careless mistakes: misspellings, leaving out words, typing words twice in a row, and so forth. Before you turn your paper in, proofread it carefully.

PUTTING IT ALL TOGETHER
• •

Imagine that you need to evaluate and make a recommendation for a photocopier for your employer. You work in a small retail company that has 20 employees. You copy correspondence, sales reports, and inter-office memos. Your office makes about 250 photocopies every day. Though most of your copying jobs are small, you do copy quarterly sales reports, which average 100 pages of originals and are sent to 50 people.

On the next page, examine the qualities of two photocopiers you are considering.

PhotoMagic 2000	CopyMatic 420
Contact Information:	Contact Information:
Pat Margolis, Sales Mgr.	Juan Mendez, Sales Mgr.
PhotoMagic, Inc.	CopyMatic, Inc.
2100 Park Way	1400 Main Street
Springfield, OH 43210	Freetown, NY 01234
Price: $2,300	Price: $3,100
Features: automatic feeder, sorter, and stapler; two-sided copying; reduction and enlargement; password entry (up to 25 passwords)	Features: automatic feeder and sorter; two-sided copying; reduction and enlargement; password entry (up to 50 passwords)
Capacity: standard paper tray holds 2,500 sheets of paper; alternate tray holds 250; feeder holds 50 originals; machine will sort 20 copies	Capacity: standard paper tray holds 5,000 sheets of paper; alternate tray holds 150; feeder holds 75 originals; machine will sort 25 copies
Speed: warm-up period is 3 minutes after the machine is turned on; makes 40 copies per minute	Speed: warm-up period is 2 minutes after the machine is turned on; makes 50 copies per minute
Service contract: free service for the first year, $150 yearly afterwards, and $25 per service visit	Service contract: free service for the first six months, $500 yearly afterwards, and no charge for service calls

1. Write a memo to your boss recommending one of the photo-copiers. Explain your choice clearly by comparing the features that are important to your business. Use proper memo format.

2. Write a letter to the sales manager of the company whose copier you have chosen. In your letter, ask for more information about the product. Indicate that you would like to have a demonstration of the machine and how it works, and you would like to have information about the average service performance of the machine (that is, how many times the machine breaks down in a year, on average). If you have other questions or comments to add to your letter, include them. Be sure to use proper business letter format and a proper form of address.

Test-Taking Tip

Prepare for open-book tests to help you perform better. During open-book tests, or tests for which you may use notes and books, many students find themselves spending more time reading through the material they have brought to the test than answering the questions on the test. Here are some things you can do to prepare for an open-book test:

- Use sticky notes to mark pages with important information.

- Write summary notes in the margins or on sheets of paper inserted into the book.

- Organize any notes you are using and mark important sections with a highlighting pen.

- Mark quotations or passages you are likely to use from your reading.

- Write key definitions or information on flash cards for easy reference.

CHECK YOUR PROGRESS

On a scale of 1 to 5, rate how well you have mastered the goals set at the beginning of the chapter:

1 2 3 4 5   understand and use proper writing formats in workplace communication.

1 2 3 4 5   understand the appropriate types of address required in business writing.

1 2 3 4 5   consider your career options early to help you choose the right courses in school.

1 2 3 4 5   use rules to avoid mistakes in spelling.

1 2 3 4 5   (your own goal) _____

1 2 3 4 5   (your own goal) _____

If you've given yourself a 3 or lower on any of these goals:

- visit the *Tapestry* web site for additional practice.

- ask your instructor for extra help.

- review the sections of the chapter that you found difficult.

- work with a partner or study group to further your progress.

APPENDIX 1: COMMONLY MISSPELLED, MISUSED, AND CONFUSED WORDS

accommodate	disappear	indict	o'clock
acquaint	disappoint	indispensable	offense
acquire	dissatisfied	irresistible	omitted
address	eighth	judgment*	paid
already	embarrass	laboratory	parallel
all right	environment	laugh	phenomenon
argument	equipped	league	physician
athletic	especially	library	pneumonia
auxiliary	exaggerate	license	possess
beginning	exceed	literature	potato
believe	existence	lying	preferred
bureau	fascinate	maintenance	privilege
burglar	February	maneuver	probably
calendar	foreign	mattress	psychology
ceiling	forty	mischief	raspberry
cemetery	fragile	missionary	receipt
changeable	freight	misspell	receive
chief	gauge	mortgage	recognize
circuit	government	mosquitoes	recommend
concede	grammar	necessary	resemblance
conceive	guarantee	neighbor	reservoir
counterfeit	handkerchief	niece	rhythm
debt	harass	noticeable	ridiculous
definite	height	nuisance	sandwich
dependent	heir	obedience	scissors
desperate	hygiene	occasion	secretary
develop	hypocrisy	occur	seize
devise	independence	occurred	separate

*The preferred American English spelling is *judgment*. British English spells this word *judgement*, a spelling that has some acceptance in American writing as well.

siege	succeed	truly	Wednesday
similar	success	Tuesday	weird
sincerely	supersede	usually	withhold
special	tariff	vaccinate	yolk
squirrel	threshold	vacuum	
straight	tobacco	vinegar	
strengthen	tomatoes	warrant	

COMMONLY CONFUSED WORDS

If you use any of these words in your writing, be sure you are using the right one:

accept/except	its/it's
affect/effect	lose/loose
capital/capitol	precede/proceed
cereal/serial	principal/principle
compliment/complement	quiet/quite
conscience/conscious	stationary/stationery
dessert/desert	than/then
formerly/formally	their/there/they're
forth/fourth	to/too/two
idol/idle	whose/who's
incite/insight	you're/your

APPENDIX 2: DOCUMENTING SOURCES

This appendix presents two different citation formats: one for writing in the humanities and one for the social sciences. There are many other formats. You will find a list of references for other format types at the end of this appendix. You should use each type appropriately, depending on your paper, and your teacher's instructions. The following outline shows only the basic elements of these two formats. For more complete instructions, refer to the *MLA Handbook for Writers of Research Papers,* 4th ed. New York: MLA, 1995, or to the *Publication Manual of the American Psychological Association*, 4th ed. Washington, DC: APA, 1994.

All formats have two basic parts: referencing within the text, used when quoting, and a list of sources, known generally as a bibliography or reference list. Specific citation formats may have additional features.*

◇ Humanities: MLA Format

MLA stands for "Modern Language Association," and its format is the preferred style for writing in literature.

Quotation References

When you quote or refer to an author within your text, you should include a **parenthetical reference**. Within the parentheses, include the author's last name and the page number on which you found the reference. Look carefully at the punctuation conventions as well. Even if you only summarize or paraphrase another author, you still must give a reference:

> "Philosophy since Kant," he argues, "has purported to be a science which could sit in judgment on all the other sciences" (Rorty 141).

If you are quoting more than one source by the same author, then you need to include a shortened title as well.

> As Prichard writes, "Everything turns upon how the principles of criticism are applied" (Prichard, <u>Practical Critical Practice</u> 121).

When any of the information normally put within the parentheses is included in your sentence, you can omit that part from the citation.

> In <u>Principles of American Literary Criticism</u>, Prichard notes that the "theory of language is the most neglected of all studies" (261).

When you quote a longer passage (usually more than three lines of your paper), that quotation should be indented and offset from the rest of the text. Notice in the previous examples that the parenthetical reference comes before the final punctuation instead of after. Do not put quotation marks around a block quotation.

---

*Many of the references used in this chapter are fictitious; don't use them to conduct your own research.

In his essay, he writes:

I am not sure that "phase two" marks a split with "phase one," a split whose form would be cut along an indivisible line. The relationship between these two phases doubtless has another structure. (Derrida 72)

If you omit part of a quotation, you should signal this omission with an **ellipsis,** . . . a series of three dots. If you need to rephrase a portion of the author's words or add a word in order to maintain the phrase's grammaticality or sense in the quotation, you can do so with **square brackets** [ ]. You should never omit important information or rephrase the author's words in a manner that changes the original meaning.

According to Tanaka, critical reading "should offer a means of inducing constant habits of feeling . . . [and] the possibility of one's acting in accordance with the findings of one's improved intelligence" (29).

If the portion of text you omit is at the end of a sentence, you need to add a fourth dot, which is actually the final punctuation of the sentence.

Wang notes that "every statement makes a claim to justice, sincerity, beauty, and truthfulness. . . . And these values are not defined by their relation to language, but by their relation to reality . . ." (123).

If there are two authors, they should be referenced in the order they appear on the cover of the book or in the title of the work.

"American New Criticism also tended to surpass the British in the degree to which it was willing to formulate the objective form of poetry" (Davis and Schleifer 79).

If there are three authors, you should use the following form:

Paton himself demonstrated that children's difficulties with conservation of length could be lessened by weakening the visual illusion involved (Paton, Regis, and Szeminska 43).

If there are more than three authors in the text, list the first author, then the abbreviation *et al.* (meaning "and others") and the page number.

The authors found no difference in the two situations (Terrace et al. 1891).

Some Special Cases

If your work does not have an author listed, use a shortened version of the title in the parenthetical reference.

("Bridges in the Night" 1911).

If the entire reference is only one page long, you do not need to list a page number in the parentheses.

When something you read refers to another source, and you do not read the source referred to, use the abbreviation *qtd.* ("quoted") as part of your reference.

Miller said that literature and history "were inextricably entwined" (qtd. in James 15).

When you support a claim with more than one reference, cite each work as previously specified, but separate them with semicolons.

(Martin 123; Garcia 99).

If two authors you refer to have the same last name, include their first names or initials to distinguish them.

(John Smith 41) and (G. E. Smith 23).

If you are referring to a novel or a poem, it is helpful to give more information about where you found your information. You may include a chapter number.

In <u>A Tale of Two Cities</u>, Dickens begins with a very long sentence (1; Chapter 1).

If you refer to, or copy, an author's figure or table, you must include that information at the bottom of the graphic material. Format the source line like this:

Source: Raul Jimenez, "A Guide to Poetry," <u>Journal of Poetry 8</u> (1934): 33.

Source List

Every citation that you list in a parentheses in your text must appear, in alphabetical order by authors' last names, in a section called <u>Works Cited</u>, which you place at the end of your paper. If you also want to include titles of works you read but did not reference directly in your paper, you should call your list <u>Works Consulted</u>. In general, in your bibliography you should underline the titles of books and other major works, but put double quotation marks around the titles of smaller works, such as articles, short stories, and poems.

Books

The basic entry for each book listing in your bibliography is made up of the following: the author's name, followed by a period and two spaces; the title, underlined and followed by a period and two spaces; the city of publication,* followed by a colon and two spaces; the name of the publisher, followed by a comma; and the year of publication, followed by a period. The second line and any line after it in each reference should be indented.

Yeats, William Butler. <u>Collected Poems</u>. New York: Macmillan, 1956.

If the book has an **edition number,** that information should come after the title, followed by a period.

Yeats, William Butler. <u>Collected Poems</u>. 2nd ed. New York: Macmillan, 1958.

*If the city of publication is small or not well-known, and if it is a U.S. publisher, include the state as well. If the publisher is outside the United States and the city of publication is small or lesser known, include the country name.

When the book has more than two or three authors, only the first author has the order of his or her name reversed. Enter the names in the same order that they appear on the title page of the book.

Marx, Karl, and Friedrich Engels. <u>Capital: A Critique of Political Economy</u>. New York: Vintage, 1976.

When the book has three or more authors, use the abbreviation *et al.* (see the explanation on page 209).

Smith, Michael, et al. <u>The Many Uses of Masking Tape</u>. New York: Walkabout, 1991.

If you refer to two or more books by the same author, include the author's name only in the first entry. After that, use three dashes (---) followed by a period in place of the author's name. List the books, in this case, alphabetically by the title.

Norris, Christopher. <u>Derrida</u>. Cambridge: Harvard UP, 1987.
---. <u>Paul de Man</u>. New York: Routledge, 1988.

If you refer to a specific volume (or volumes) of a multi-volume work, include the volume number in your reference, along with the total number of volumes available.

Smetana, Susan. Vol. 4 of <u>A History of Nylon Carpets</u>. 16 vols. Muncie, IN: IAP, 1992.

If the book you cite has an editor rather than an author, the citation form depends upon the information you use. If you use materials written by the editor, such as notes, introduction, foreword, and so forth, then refer to the editor in your bibliography.

Kovacs, Pilar, ed. <u>For and Against: Famous Arguments</u>. New Brighton, MN: Snowpress, 1955.

However, if you are mostly concerned with the original material and don't refer to the editor's remarks, list it by the author's name.

Ruetz, Anna. <u>For and Against: Famous Arguments</u>. Ed. Pilar Kovacs. New Brighton, MN: Snowpress, 1955.

If you use one essay or work out of a collection, list the individual essay, not the entire book. You will need to include the relevant page numbers as well.

Sikorsky, Elena. "Big and Little Ideas." <u>Catalogue of Different Theories</u>. Ed. Bobby McGee. Paris: Voila, 1994. 110–115.

The preface, foreword, afterword, or introduction to a book must be referenced if you cite it. Write the appropriate term before the title, followed by a period.

Bolling, Simon. Introduction. <u>Beginning Dutch</u>. By Hans Hollander. The Hague: The Press, 1983. i–xiv.*

*If the page numbers are Roman in the original text, you must use Roman numerals in your citation as well.

If you are using a translation, list the translator's name after the title, using the abbreviation "Trans."

> Molina, Antonia. <u>Life and Death on Russian Hill</u>. Trans. Paula Herrera. San Francisco: Angel, 1906.

If you use an encyclopedia, you do not need to include the volume and page numbers. For major encyclopedias, you do not need to include publication information, either. If the item from the encyclopedia does not have an author, list it under the title of the entry.

> "Ellis Island." <u>Encyclopedia Americana</u>. 1988 ed.

If an author or authors are listed for the entry, include the name(s) as you would any other entry. If you use a smaller, less well-known encyclopedia, you should include publication information.

When you use a government document and no author is listed, use the name of the government agency in place of the author's name.

> United States Dept. of Agriculture. <u>Six Hundred Species of Garden Peas</u>. Washington, DC: GPO, 1933.

Articles

A citation to an article contains the following information: the author's name, followed by a period and two spaces; the title, followed by a period, enclosed in quotation marks and followed by two spaces; the title of the periodical, underlined and followed by the volume number; the date of publication in parentheses, followed by a colon and a space; and the full page numbers* of the article, followed by a period.

A professional journal:

> LeMonde, Alain R. "French Bicycles Throughout History." <u>Journal of Bicycle Studies</u> 14 (1984): 21–39.

When you refer to an author's review of another writer's work, include the phrase *"Rev. of"* by the work that is reviewed, and then after the title, the phrase *by* plus the original author's name.

> Smith, Chris. Rev. of <u>A Tale of Two Cities</u>, by Charles Dickens. <u>The Annual Review of Really Old Books</u> 14 (1995): 23–35.

A popular magazine:

1. Weekly: List the complete date and page numbers.

> Walla, Jamal. "A Word on Patios." <u>New Jersey Life</u> 13 Oct. 1989: 56+.

2. Monthly: Include only the month and year. Do not include volume or issue numbers.

> Thomsen, Paul. "Life on Fiji." <u>Travel Today</u> May 1988: 19–21.

---

*If an article does not appear on consecutive pages—that is, if there are "skips" in the printing—state the first page number of the article, followed by a plus sign (40+, for example, for an article beginning on page 40).

If an article in a magazine has no author, list it alphabetically by the title.

A newspaper: List the name of the newspaper as it appears on the first page, without any articles to start it (for example, <u>San Francisco Chronicle</u>, not <u>The San Francisco Chronicle</u>). Give the date it appeared, the edition (found at the top of the front page), and if the sections are numbered or lettered, that information along with the page numbers.

> Carman, John. "'Tales' a San Francisco Treat." <u>San Francisco Chronicle</u> 10 Jan. 1994, final ed.: sec. D: 1–2.

If the item is an editorial, include the word "Editorial" followed by a period, after the title. Again, if there is no author identified, use the title as the item to list.

> "State Needs Help to Pay Alien Costs." Editorial. <u>San Francisco Chronicle</u> 10 Jan. 1994, final ed.: sec. A: 22.

If you want to cite a letter to the editor, include the word "Letter" after the author's name.

> Sias, Laura. Letter. <u>San Francisco Chronicle</u> 10 Jan. 1994, final ed.: sec. A: 22.

Nonprint References

Films and videos: You may use different formats for citing films and videos, depending on whom or what you wish to emphasize. (For example, you can list one by the director's name, if that is important to your paper.) However, it is probably simplest to list all video and films by their titles. Include date and production information, including the director's name.

> <u>Annie Hall</u>. Dir. Woody Allen. United Artists, 1977.

Personal interviews:

> Jordan, Michael. Personal interview. 21 Jan. 1993.
> Barkley, Charles. Telephone interview. 14 Dec. 1992.

Lectures: Include the name of the lecturer, the title, location, and date. If there was a sponsor or series name, include that as well. If the lecture has no title, provide a descriptive name yourself.

> Lao, Pufang. "The Cultural Revolution." Asian Studies Colloquium, Dept. of Chinese, University of Illinois, 23 June 1986.

Personal letters: If you want to quote a letter someone wrote to you, refer to yourself as "the author":

> Clinton, Bill. Letter to the author. 20 Feb. 1993.

Information from a computer service: Cite this information just as you would an article, but include the name of the file and any identifying numbers with it.

> Jersey, Delia. "The Newest Information Trends." <u>Information News Weekly</u>, 10 Aug. 1985: 121+. INFONET file 22a, item 85.08.10.

Computer software: Include the company that produced the software, the title of the program, and the year of publication. Also include the type of machine for which it was written.

SimFarm. Computer Software. Maxis, 1993. IBM.

An Internet Site: Include author, date, title and other information to identify the site. Include the full internet address.

Jobs, Steve. "Apple, Apple, Apple."
http://www.apple.com/apple.html June 1999.

Television/Radio: Record the underlined name of the program, the network or cable station that produced it or showed it, the local station, city, and date of the program.

New Horizons in Bonsai. KCSM-60, San Mateo. 11 Jan. 1994.

MLA style also allows explanatory notes. If you need to include information that doesn't fit clearly into your text or doesn't use a standard reference citation, include it in a note. Number these notes sequentially in your paper, and then list them on a separate page at the end of your paper just before your *Works Cited* list.

In your paper:

Television has reached new heights of violence, according to some experts.[1]

On your "Notes" page:

[1]For more information about recent polls, see the article "The Real Story of Violence," in *TV Guide,* January 1, 1994.

Social Sciences: APA Format

The American Psychological Association (APA) format is a popular format for the social sciences and other areas of research. It uses short references, including the last name of the authors and the year of publication, put within parentheses inserted in the text. The following references are the same as those in the MLA section, but they have been changed to the APA format.

APA also uses **parenthetical reference.** It is different from MLA in that a comma is used in the parentheses.

"Philosophy since Kant," he argues, "has purported to be a science which could sit in judgment on all the other sciences" (Rorty, 1976, p. 141).

If you are quoting more than one source by the same author, the date usually tells the one to which you are referring. However, if the author has two different publications in the same year, in your reference list and your citations follow the year date with the letters *a* for the first one, *b* for the second, so on, alphabetized according to the title.

As Prichard writes, "Everything turns upon how the principles of criticism are applied" (Prichard, 1991a, p. 121).

When any of the information normally put within the parentheses is included in your sentence, you can omit that part from the citation.

In <u>Principles of American Literary Criticism</u>, Prichard notes that the "theory of language is the most neglected of all studies" (199lb, p. 261).

When you quote a longer passage (more than 40 words), that quotation should be indented and offset from the rest of the text. Notice that the parenthetical reference comes after the final punctuation. Do not put quotation marks around block quotations.

In his review, Genovese writes:

> In the comparative balance of opportunities and rewards for males and females, the role of money receives the stress it deserves in this work. If there is truth in the motto "In vino, veritas" it might be useful to add another, "In moneta, status." (1999, p. 144)

If you omit part of a quotation, you should signal this omission with an **ellipsis**. See the instructions in the previous section on page 209.

If there are from two to six authors, they should be referenced in the order they appear on the cover of the book or in the title of the work, and joined with an ampersand (&).

> "American New Criticism also tended to surpass the British in the degree to which it was willing to formulate the objective form of poetry" (Davis & Schleifer, 1991, p. 21).

If there are more than six authors in the text, list the first author and then the abbreviation *et al.* (meaning "and others").

> The authors found no difference in the two situations (Terrace et al., 1891).

Some Special Cases

If your work does not have an author listed, use a shortened version of the title in the parenthetical reference.

> ("Bridges in the Night," 1911).

When something you read refers to another source, and you do not read that source, use the phrase 'cited in' as part of your reference.

> Miller said that literature and history "were inextricably entwined" (cited in James, 1991, p. 15).

When you support a claim with more than one reference, cite each work as previously specified, but separate them with semicolons. List them in alphabetical order.

> (Garcia, 1982; Martin, 1923).

If two authors you cite have the same last name, include their initials to distinguish them.

> (J. Smith, 1941) and (G. E. Smith, 1923).

If you are referring to a novel or a poem, it is helpful to give more information about where you found your information. You may include a chapter number. Abbreviate words such as "section" and "chapter."

> In <u>A Tale of Two Cities</u>, Dickens begins with a very long sentence (1900; chap. 1).

If you refer to, or copy, an author's figure or table, you must include that information at the bottom of the graphic material. Use the following format:

Source: Jimenez, 1934, p. 33.

Source List

Every citation that you list in a parentheses in your text must appear, in alphabetical order by author's last names, in a section called <u>References</u>, which you place at the end of your paper. In general, in your reference list, you should underline the titles of books and other major works, but do not put double quotation marks around the titles of smaller works, such as articles, short stories, and poems. In titles, capitalize only the first letter of the first word, first letters of proper nouns, and the first letter of the first word after a colon.

Books

The basic entry for each book listing in your bibliography is made up of the following: the author's last name, followed by his or her initials; the year of publication in parentheses, followed by a period and two spaces; the title, underlined and followed by a period and two spaces; the city of publication,* followed by a colon and then the name of the publisher, followed by a period. The second line and those following should be indented.

Yeats, W. B. (1956). <u>Collected poems</u>. New York: Macmillan.

If the book has an **edition** number, that information should come after the title, in parentheses and followed by a period.

Yeats, W. B. (1956). <u>Collected poems</u> (2nd ed.). New York: Macmillan.

When the book has more than two to six authors, all authors have the order of their names reversed. Enter the names in the same order that they appear on the title page of the book.

Marx, K., & Engels, F. (1976). <u>Capital: A Critique of Political Economy</u>. New York: Vintage, 1976.

When the book has three or more authors, use the abbreviation *et al.* (see page 209).

Smith, M., et al. (1991). <u>The Many Uses of Masking Tape</u>. New York: Walkabout.

If you refer to a specific volume (or volumes) of a multi-volume work, include the volume number in your reference.

*If the city of publication is small or not well-known, and if it is a U.S. publisher, include the state as well. If the publisher is outside the United States and the city of publication is small or lesser known, include the country name.

Smetana, S. (1992). <u>A History of Nylon Carpets: Vol. 4</u>. Muncie, IN: IAP.

If the book you cite has an editor, and you want to refer to the editor's comments rather than an author, use the following organization.

Kovacs, P. (Ed.). (1955). Introduction. In A. Ruetz, <u>For and Against: Famous Arguments</u>. New Brighton, MN: Snowpress.

If you use one essay or work out of a collection, list the individual essay, not the entire book. You will need to include the relevant page numbers as well.

Sikorsky, E. (1994). Big and Little Ideas. In B. McGee (Ed.), <u>Catalogue of Different Theories</u> (pp. 110–115). Paris: Voila Press.

If you are using a translation, list the translator's name after the author's name (in parentheses) using the abbreviation "Trans."

Molina, A. (D. Ferina, Trans.). (1906). <u>Life and Death on Russian Hill</u>. San Francisco: Angel.

If you use an encyclopedia, you need to include the volume and page number, and include publication information as well. If the item from the encyclopedia does not have an author, list it under the title of the entry.

Ellis Island. (1988). <u>Encyclopedia Americana</u> (Vol. 4, pp. 300–344). New York: Americana.

If there is an author or authors listed for the entry, include their names as you would any other entry. If you use a government document, and there is no author listed, use the name of the government agency as the author. Include the government document number.

United States Dept. of Agriculture. (1933). <u>Six Hundred Species of Garden Peas</u>. (NTIS No. P880-14333). Washington, DC: U.S. Government Printing Office.

Articles

A citation to an article contains the following information: the author's name (last name, initials), followed by a period and two spaces; the year of publication in parentheses, followed by a period and two spaces; the title of the article, followed by a period and two spaces; the title of the periodical, followed by a comma; the volume number, underlined and followed by a comma; and the full page numbers* of the article, followed by a period. The first line is indented.

A professional journal:

NOTE: All major words in a journal or magazine name should be capitalized.

*If an article does not appear on consecutive pages—that is, if there are "skips" in the printing—give all page numbers, separated by commas—for example, pp. 40, 42, 44–47.

LeMonde, A. R. (1984). French Bicycles Throughout History. The Journal of Bicycle Studies, 14, 21–39.

When you refer to an author's review of another writer's work, include the phrase *"Rev. of"* by the work that is reviewed, and then after the title, the phrase *by* plus the original author's name.

Smith, C. (1995). An Old Favorite. [Rev. of A Tale of Two Cities, by Charles Dickens] The Annual Review of Really Old Books, 14, 23–35.

A popular magazine:

Weekly: List the complete date and page numbers.

Walla, J. (1989, October 13). A Word on Patios. New Jersey Life, pp. 56–78.

Monthly: Include only the month and year. Do not include volume or issue numbers.

Thomsen, P. (1988, May). Life on Fiji. Travel Today, pp. 19–21.

If an article in a magazine has no author identified, list it alphabetically by the title.

A newspaper: List the name of the newspaper as it appears on the first page, without any articles to start it (for example, San Francisco Chronicle, not The San Francisco Chronicle). Give the date it appeared, the edition (found at the top of the front page), and if the sections are numbered or lettered, that information along with the page numbers. If the pages are not consecutive, give all the page numbers, separated by commas.

Carman, J. (1994, January 10). 'Tales' a San Francisco Treat. San Francisco Chronicle, pp. D1–D2.

If you want to cite a letter to the editor, include the word "Letter" after the author's name.

Sias, L. Letter. (1994, January 10). In Support of Bosnian Intervention. San Francisco Chronicle, p. A22.

Nonprint References

Films and videos:

Allen, W. (Director) & Joffe, C. H. (Producer). (1977). Annie Hall [Film]. Culver City, CA: United Artists.

Personal interviews: Unpublished interviews should not be listed in your references. Instead, explain the interview in your text, or in a note.

Published interviews:

Smart, J. (1993, January 21). [Interview with Michael Jordan]. Sports Illustrated, p. 34.

Information from a computer service: Cite this information just as you would an article, but include the name of the file and any identifying numbers with it.

Jersey, D. (1985, August 10). The newest information trends. Information News Weekly, pp. 121, 123, 135. [INFONET file 22a, item 85.08.10].

Computer software: Include the company that produced the software, the title of the program, and the year of publication. Also include the type of machine for which it is written.

SimFarm. (1993). [Computer Software]. Orinda, CA: Maxis. IBM.

An Internet site: Include author, date, title, and other information to identify the site. Include full internet address.

Jobs, S. (1999, June). Apple, Apple, Apple.
http://www.apple.com/apple.html

APA style also allows explanatory notes. If you need to include information that doesn't fit clearly into your text or doesn't use a standard reference citation, include it in a note. Number these notes sequentially in your paper, and then list them on a separate page at the end of your paper that you place just before your References list.

In your paper:

Television has reached new heights of violence, according to some experts.[1]

On your "Notes" page:

[1]For more information about recent polls, see the article "The Real Story of Violence" in TV Guide, January 1, 1994.

References to Other Style Guides

American Chemical Society. Handbook for Authors of Papers in the American Chemical Society Publications. Washington: American Chemical Soc., 1978.

American Institute of Physics. Style Manual for Guidance in the Preparation of Papers. 3rd ed. New York: American Inst. of Physics, 1978.

The Chicago Manual of Style. 13th ed. Chicago: University of Chicago Press, 1982.

Council of Biological Editors. CBE Style Manual. 5th ed. Bethesda, MD: CBE, 1983.

Irvine, Demar B. Writing About Music: A Style Book for Reports and Theses. Seattle: Univ. of Washington Press, 1968.

Turabian, Kate L. A Manual for Writers of Term Papers, Theses, and Dissertations. Chicago: Univ. of Chicago Press, 1973.

SKILLS INDEX

PHOTO CREDITS

• •